Keith Lamdin is Director of Stewardship, Training, Evangelism and Ministry in the Diocese of Oxford.

David Tilley has worked in the training of Methodist Ministers, and in Continuing Ministerial Education of clergy in the Coventry Diocese. He was awarded an MPhil in 2006 following empirical research on the training of curates of the Church of England.

SUPPORTING NEW MINISTERS IN THE LOCAL CHURCH

A Handbook

SPCK Library of Ministry

KEITH LAMDIN AND DAVID TILLEY

First published in Great Britain in 2007
Society for Promoting Christian Knowledge
36 Causton Street
London SW1P 4ST

SPCK does not necessarily endorse the individual views contained in its publications.

On p. 143, Alan Wilson's biblical models of supervision are used with permission and
the authors are grateful to him for allowing the inclusion of his article as Appendix 1;
extracts from *Into Deep Water* by Neil Burgess, on p. 27, are reproduced by permission
of Kevin Mayhew Ltd, Licence Nr. 601142; on p. 60, the description of learning styles
from *Learning for Life* (Yvonne Craig, 1994), is used with the kind permission of
Continuum International Publishing Group; Figure 6.1 on p. 71 is adapted from
Fig. 11.2, p. 148, in *Reflection and Learning in Professional Development*, Jennifer Moon
(Kogan Page, 1999); we are grateful to Professor Leslie Francis for permission to
include the Francis Psychological Type Scales in Appendix 2; Appendix 4 and
Appendix 5 are taken from *Shaping the Future: New Patterns of Training for Lay
and Ordained* (Church House Publishing), © The Archbishops' Council 2006,
reproduced by permission.

Every effort has been made to acknowledge fully the sources of material reproduced
in this book. The publisher apologizes for any omissions that may remain and,
if notified, will ensure that full acknowledgements are made in a subsequent edition.

Scripture quotations are from the New Revised Standard Version of the Bible,
Anglicized Edition, copyright © 1989, 1995 by the Division of Christian Education
of the National Council of the Churches of Christ in the USA. Used by permission.
All rights reserved.

British Library Cataloguing-in-Publication Data
A catalogue record for this book is available from the British Library

ISBN 978–0–281–05879–2

1 3 5 7 9 10 8 6 4 2

Typeset by Graphicraft Limited, Hong Kong
Printed in Great Britain by Ashford Colour Printers

Produced on paper from sustainable forests

*This book is dedicated to unsung heroes and heroines
of the Church of England – the training incumbents –
who take on extra work and responsibility and who
will help to shape the next generation of leaders in
the Church. We hope this book will enable them to be
more confident and to find the role more
fulfilling and rewarding.*

Contents

Contents

Contents

Foreword

This book is written to help those who are given the responsibility of providing leadership and supervision for newly ordained ministers.

It explores, in a religious context, what supervision means, and the models and understandings that will underpin good practice. It offers advice on how to set up and maintain supervision with a professional colleague, and how to deal with some common problems.

Although neither of the authors has himself been a training incumbent they draw on their experience of having oversight for the growth and development of curates of two dioceses of the Church of England, and the responsibility for training their supervisors.

Much may be familiar to experienced training incumbents who nevertheless may find it helpful to have it presented coherently in one volume. To those who are new to the role it offers a comprehensive guide to the effective steering into ordained ministry and the supervision of newly ordained colleagues.

What all will find new are the conclusions which arise from research with curates that David Tilley conducted for an MPhil degree. Between 2000 and 2004 over a hundred curates, whose psychological types and those of their incumbents were known, completed a questionnaire. The findings based on these data will provide readers with insight into what curates say works for them, and what helps them to grow into leadership at a crucial time for the Church of England.

Acknowledgements

We owe a debt of gratitude to many people, many of whom are unaware of it. We would like to acknowledge our thanks to all who have helped in our learning, especially the colleagues with whom we have worked and learned so much.

We would like to thank all the curates and training incumbents who have worked with us, whose questions have fostered our own reflective practice.

We are particularly grateful for the comments and opinions we have received and used in preparing this book – the curates whose experience and words we quote, and ministers in secular employment, and others who have taken the trouble to offer us their views.

We are also grateful to Professor Leslie Francis for permission to use the Francis Psychological Type Scales and the opportunity to offer readers' insights from his questionnaire included in Appendix 2.

We are particularly grateful to those who have encouraged and helped in the production of the text – to Andrew Gear (who now holds responsibility for training supervising incumbents in Oxford diocese), to Elizabeth Mitchell and Eric Johnson for proof-reading, to Tammy James and Trisha Dale for polishing and editing the final document. We would also like to thank Ruth McCurry of SPCK for her encouragement and invaluable advice.

Keith Lamdin and David Tilley

1

Introduction: what is supervision?

You have a recently ordained colleague coming. You will be expected to guide the newly ordained through entry into ordained ministry, to oversee his or her work and to facilitate continued learning in the next three or four years.

- How are you going to think about it?
- How would describe what you think you will be doing?
- What will you be – teacher? manager? leader? trainer? supervisor? wise elder friend?
- What pressures do you anticipate?

And perhaps the most important questions:

- What was it like for you as a curate?
- And what kind of experience of supervision do you have now?
- What has been good practice that you would want to employ?
- What has been bad that you would want to avoid?

This book is designed to help those who supervise new ministers immediately after their ordination. We hope that Anglican training incumbents, supervising Methodist ministers and others to whom is given the oversight of newly commissioned ministers will find this book helpful. It will offer ideas for good practice, possibilities for solving problems and a number of different models of adult learning and supervision, together with suggestions for practical ways of working together with a curate. While this book is focused on Anglican curates because this is our area of expertise, we anticipate that it will have much wider application: ordinands on placement, newly appointed youth ministers and pastoral assistants, newly licensed and authorized preachers, readers and lay ministers in all denominations. We hope that readers will be willing to make the appropriate translation for their own context where we offer illustrations from the church with which we are most familiar.

Even more than this narrow but essential focus, it is possible to think of the primary role of ministers as supervising the development and growth of all the baptized, not only as volunteers within the life of the church, but also in their discipleship in the world. It is possible to coin the phrase, within Anglicanism, 'every incumbent a training incumbent'.

In the last 50 years or so the Church's ideas about curates have developed significantly. No longer are curates seen primarily as another pair of hands that hopefully will learn on the job, chiefly by watching and copying. A number of reasons make the current situation one of urgent need for good practice.

- There are few, if any, second curacies. An extended and leisurely entry into self-managed and self-motivated ministry is no longer available.
- The boundary between pre- and post-ordination learning for ministry is seen as less important, as lifelong learning becomes the norm for all ministers.
- There has been a parallel rise in the knowledge and application of adult learning theory in this same period.
- Professional supervision and mentoring is accepted as normative in other professions, such as medicine, nursing, social work, probation and legal practice, as people come to expect consistently high standards from all sectors of public life. The Church has no less a need for professional competence in the supervision of new clergy, and has much to learn as well as to share in this area.
- Newly ordained ministers are often entering a second profession and bring with them experience and expectations of supervision from their previous working life.

However, there are some factors that make the situation of clergy and other ministers distinctive. There are few rules and regulations about professional ministry, and ministers do not work regular hours and find it difficult to set aside time when they are 'off duty'. Ministers work from home much of the time and have complex boundaries to manage between home, work and time for each. Ministers deal with high and low points of human experience when emotions can be intense. Things of the spirit are the currency with which they work. Ministers work with human relationships, sometimes at their rawest. They are themselves fallible beings who, at times, struggle with their own relating, their faith and doubts, and to live lives consistent with following Jesus Christ.

At the same time ministers, like all people in leadership, are always experiencing the projections and dependency needs that come from both those they lead and from the general public. While this is not the book to explore these in depth, and although people in social care experience similar things, the way these dependencies operate in the religious and spiritual sphere can be alarming to new ministers.

It has become a truism to state that society is changing at an ever-increasing rate. However, the place of religion in society, and the relationship of Christianity and its churches to other faiths, in an increasingly consumer-oriented world, has forced major changes in the mindset of the Church, and the Church of England in particular. Social forces have led to a reappraisal of the style and practice of ordained ministry. The role of the minister is more uncertain and more marginalized, and this can easily undermine enthusiasm, self-esteem and confidence.

The title of this book is *Supporting New Ministers in the Local Church*, and so some ideas about leadership in today's Church are appropriate. Ministerial leadership is remarkably imprecise and unbounded when compared, for example, with leadership in industry, commerce or the sporting world. Leaders in those fields know what it is they have to accomplish and with whom they have to work, the team they lead. It is less obvious and less precise in the Church, and subject to varying theological frames of reference and interpretation.

The modern Church has placed an emphasis on gifting and using the natural abilities created in us by a loving and generous God. Selecting which people to ask to do specific jobs is a difficult (and risky) matter of discernment. Creating the appropriate organization in the local church, or modifying that inherited from a predecessor, requires judgement and some knowledge of management models, even if that knowledge is rudimentary. There are also issues of personality and attitude and personal chemistry to be taken into account. Further, what is meant by 'the work of building the Kingdom of God' is subject to debate and discussion and to examination from deeply held beliefs. A minister may exercise leadership in a local church as much by a quiet conversation with a few people after a service as with presentations at the Parochial Church Council (PCC) or annual church meeting.

We live in a world where what is measurable has become increasingly the way in which we apportion value. Concern with targets, goals, and cost analysis have become dominant in the world of education and health care for example, yet the work of the Kingdom, which grows secretly, and spiritual and human growth, are difficult to subject to these sorts of measurements.

Thus it is that the leadership of an incumbent, priest or minister in a local church may be much harder to assess and teach than in other fields. Ministry is not capable of being subjected to arithmetical processes, which is not to say that we should avoid any examination of what we are doing and its effect on individuals and communities.

All this, and more, makes the task of supervising a newly ordained minister important and a privilege; a joy, both rewarding and demanding. Supervision produces challenges that are often present in relationships with others in the local church, e.g. organist and lay minister or reader. These challenges are painted in brighter colours in the relationship between senior and junior clergy.

In order to help people in this role of supervision, in this book we draw on the wealth of material, largely written for the secular field, which has been applied to the context of the local church. We have between us well over 20 years of working with curates and training incumbents, and offer here the things we have tested and proved to be useful. Naturally, over the years, our learning has been tested and enriched by conversations with our colleagues in other dioceses and churches.

Every supervisor leads another and helps them to learn in their own distinctive way, just as every leader leads in their own way. It may be that you will find much in this book to be familiar, especially if you have experience of supervising other ministers. However, we trust that it will be useful to have it spelled out in words. In this way we expect that you will become more aware of your own natural style of supervision and so be more conscious of good practice. We offer an overview of the issues and practice of the supervision of the newly ordained, not wanting to be prescriptive or to offer a constraint to your natural style of supervision but rather to provide a forum in which you can interrogate and refine your own intuitive experience as supervisor.

What is supervision?

The word 'supervisor' is used in different ways in different settings. In a factory or a supermarket it might mean the person who wears a slightly different uniform who walks down the line to sort out problems and to make sure operators know what they should be doing, that they are doing it properly and they know when to take a break. Managerial and support components are both prominent in this use of the word.

Supervision can be used generally to embrace a number of constituent roles and functions that are the responsibility of a senior towards a junior colleague or colleagues. In the spheres of social care and counselling the word takes on a different flavour. Here it can also be used very specifically to define a relationship of support, mentoring, reflection and guidance that may or may not be a part of the managerial relationship. In this latter sense supervision is part of the professional discipline of many people who work in areas where human relations are the main content of their work.

In this book we will be using the word in the senses of both management and mentoring and will seek to make clear which sense is employed when the context does not make it obvious. We turn now to some definitions of supervision.

Hawkins and Shohet (1989) identify three integrated roles of a supervisor: these are educator, provider of support, and managerial overseer. They affirm that these do not always sit comfortably together. They also offer the definition of Hess (1980): 'a quintessentially interpersonal interaction with the general goal that one person, the supervisor, meets with another, the supervisee, in an effort to make the latter more effective in helping people.'

Bramley (1996) suggests that supervision is the process of an experienced psychotherapist helping less experienced psychotherapists to become better psychotherapists. Ward (2005) introduces the concept of giving someone 'space'; the provision of distance both in time and venue from the immediacy of day-to-day work. She expands the concept: 'a facilitating environment where experimentation with practice can happen, risks taken, dialogue be heard and creative options tried out.'

Alan Wilson (1999), now Bishop of Buckingham, describes the constituent roles applied in Oxford diocese in theological terms: 'The duties of ministerial supervision are defined by four functions; support, education, management and mediation.'

This model will be explored more thoroughly below in relation to supervising incumbents and curates. Another definition familiar in Lichfield and Coventry dioceses is offered by Mary Wilson, a professional supervisor and former chair of Lichfield's Board of Ministry: '[Supervision is] a method of working closely with an individual, for whom you have a defined responsibility, which is structured, creative, challenging and enriching and is based on mutual respect and trust.'

Enough has probably been given here to indicate the specifics of supervision which we believe are applicable to those who have the oversight of newly ordained women and men. It remains only to draw attention to the relationships between the English words supervision and oversight, and the New Testament word used to describe the function of the bishop, *episcope*. The biblical background to Alan Wilson's models of supervision is included in this book as Appendix 1.

Management, together with its associated words, is often regarded with suspicion in church circles. Nevertheless into the hands of the incumbent of a Church of England parish is placed the care of and responsibility for the cure of souls which is shared with the bishop, 'both yours and mine', the words used at the institution of a new Anglican incumbent. Thus the bishop shares his oversight with the parish priest who is both responsible for overseeing the ministry of the parish, and accountable for it to the bishop. You cannot give away the authority that has been vested in you, but you can delegate parts of it to others. Thus part of the ministerial/priestly work is delegated to the curate and other ministers who are licensed by the bishop to minister in the benefice. In this way, while the accountability to God of every priest is incarnated in the accountability of each to the bishop, the specific responsibility of the incumbent is for the whole ministry of the parish.

We offer now a more detailed description of the model given by Alan Wilson in Oxford diocese. Figure 1.1 shows that the role of

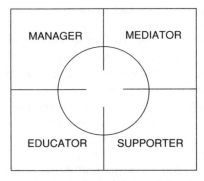

Figure 1.1 The constituent roles of the training incumbent

training incumbent integrates four constituent roles; manager, educator, mediator and supporter.

Incumbent as manager

As manager of local ministry we might see the incumbent as having a managerial responsibility towards a junior colleague. This oversight will include having responsibility for their conduct, their work and its quality and how they occupy the role as well as defining the areas and limits of the curate's authority. Decisions about the curate's pastoral responsibility for an area of the parish or a daughter church are examples of this function. Included in this role is the responsibility to give direction and to allocate work in the parish, and to see that it reaches a required quality. Other examples of responsibilities falling within this constituent role are how well and how often the curate preaches, the system for payment of expenses, the keeping of pastoral records and aspects of administration and form-filling. The incumbent as manager will need to be familiar with the national benchmarks for initial ministerial education (IME).

The theological words that might be applicable in this context would be *steward* and *shepherd*, both of which are familiar to clergy through their use in the ordination service.

Incumbent as educator

Induction into the professional ministry of the Church brings with it a responsibility to help the new curate with the knowledge, attitudes and behaviour that are consonant with ordained ministry. For the most part this involves explaining how things are done, particularly in the local parish, and enabling the gifts of the individual to emerge, to be used in ministry and to develop. Reflection on practice, the giving of advice and instruction will all form part of this function. A supervising incumbent may invite the curate to critique a funeral the incumbent has taken, and then together to critique one conducted by the curate.

The theological word applicable here is *teacher*.

Incumbent as mediator

The greater knowledge and experience of the supervising incumbent will result in a number of occasions when the senior priest will be able to point the curate to people and to organizations that will be useful not only professionally but personally for the individual. It will also on occasion mean engaging with others on behalf of the curate. Speaking to diocesan officials about the curate's housing, or to the parish treasurer about the reimbursement of expenses and protecting curates from being caught up in parish conflicts are examples of mediation.

The theological concepts applicable here are *intercessor* and *mediator*.

Incumbent as supporter

Helping another into professional ministry will also involve a caring, but dispassionate function of giving objective support. At times this might mean helping the individual to own and face up to issues that they find difficult. For example there may be an issue of conflict with someone in the parish that the curate is not acknowledging. Helping the person to analyse what is going on, both externally and internally, to determine a range of options for action, and then to make appropriate choices is part of the pastoral care of a colleague for whom one has a defined responsibility.

The theological word that corresponds here is *pastor*.

The lines dividing the constituent roles in Figure 1.1 are not complete. This indicates the complexity of the interaction between incumbent and curate which defies, at times, a rigid categorization of behaviours. In practice there will be overlap. A discussion between the two which begins with the incumbent in the role of educator, facilitating reflection on preaching, could move smoothly into one where the incumbent needs to act as a mediator, connecting the curate with a training course, or into supporter, clarifying with the preacher the relevance of personal experience. The discussion could lead to managerial decisions about whether the curate needs to preach more often, at which services and for how long.

Whichever aspect attracts you, all these functions are in the same area of helping people to learn, grow as individuals and as disciples, and to take responsibility for using their own individual gifts effectively, as they take up and fill out the role of minister. Enabling supervising incumbents to inhabit all four aspects of their role comfortably and effectively will be a major concern in the rest of this book.

Why is supervision important in the life of your church?

There are complicating factors in the life of any church. First, all individuals, whether stipendiary, paid or voluntary, are accountable to Christ for their discipleship. As well as being answerable to God, all those in public ministry, even if elected, e.g. churchwardens, and PCC members, receive their ministry from others whether it be from the bishop in the case of churchwardens, clergy and some lay ministers, or from the incumbent or the church council in the case of lay-people. There are a range of accountabilities here and they need to be set out clearly and managed effectively, without in any way undermining the primary accountability of all to Christ.

Second, no one ministers in isolation. In the ordinal the bishop urges a collegial or collaborative approach to ministry on those to be ordained. They are required by the bishop to work with their fellow priests. It is also noted again that in Anglican polity the role of the incumbent is a ministry shared with the bishop. It is conveyed to the individual at the service of institution and induction where the bishop refers to the new ministry that is being inaugurated as 'both yours and mine'.

The metaphors used at Anglican ordinations for hundreds of years are those of people in relationship, viz. watchmen, stewards, servants and shepherds etc., images which are retained in the new ordinal to accompany *Common Worship*. The functions these metaphors describe, whether they be activities of pastoral work, preaching, teaching, management or administration, are clearly activities which require healthy relationships with other people. Thus it is clear from this list of duties that the Church of England views its ordained ministry almost exclusively in terms of the relations between people.

Third, as priests/ministers we are concerned with growing people within two contexts – the life of the local church, and also the Kingdom of God. In the local church we have authority through our ordination for helping others to grow. We are concerned with growing leaders, identifying gifts and skills, giving people experience and encouraging them to take responsibility. So far as the Kingdom is concerned we are co-disciples, learners, as we follow the path of Jesus, and with all the baptized have a calling to live the gospel and share it with others.

Fourth, in today's church there is a greater emphasis on leadership, on partnership, clusters, multi-parish benefices and ministerial teams. Leadership in this context implies supervision. Delegating authority or encouraging people to take on roles and responsibilities without supervision is an abdication of our oversight.

In summary then, this chapter has described the importance of supervision for the newly ordained and introduced the definitions. It has described a model of constituent roles that are functionally distinctive while belonging together under the overarching role of supervisor. It has placed the supervision of curates in the wider context of supervision in the life of the local church. The next chapter looks at the qualities and skills desirable in supervisors.

Points for reflection

- How is your accountability to Christ for your ministry expressed in the structures of the church?
- How many people do you supervise, and who are they?
- What is your definition of supervision? Can you improve on those definitions given above?
- What do you think those you supervise think you are doing? What do they expect of you in the relationship, and how do you know?
- Which of the constituent roles is most congenial for you: manager, educator, mediator or supporter?
- In this context which do you find the most difficult?

2

Who should be a supervisor?

- What did you feel when the bishop asked you to take on a curate?
- Did you feel your ministry had been recognized and affirmed?
- Did you feel honoured, anxious, prepared, cautious . . . or what?
- What gifts do you think you will bring to supervising a curate?

In the last chapter we saw how important supervision is, first for the newly ordained and then in the life of the Church. We explored some definitions of supervision and the constituent roles of the training incumbent.

This chapter will review the characteristics and gifts that are desirable for supervisors of those new in ministry. We will look at what guidelines there are nationally for the selection of training incumbents, and introduce issues of authority.

It is a privilege to be asked to supervise a person's entry into ordained ministry. You will rightly feel that your ministry, its content and style is being affirmed. Consciously or otherwise you will be a model for ordained ministry, and that will be enormously influential in the future life of your curate. But your values, beliefs and style will be exposed in a way that may feel uncomfortable.

This book aims to encourage you, because most people find supervision a very rewarding aspect of their ministry. Curates on the whole are very positive about their first parish. Recent research with 94 curates from a number of dioceses (Tilley, 2006) reveals some positive attitudes among curates. Table 2.1 gives the figures.

Table 2.1 Curates' views of the success of their training

	Agree	?	Disagree
Reflecting on my experience I feel prepared for public ministry in the Church of England	85%	8%	7%
My training in my title parish was reasonably satisfactory overall	75%	7%	18%

Perhaps the first questions for potential training incumbents are:

- Do you remember what it was like to be a curate?
- Do you remember how you were amazed that your incumbent could even think like that, or have such a crass set of priorities?
- Do you remember just how out of date he or she seemed to be?

Perhaps you know the story, attributed to Mark Twain, about the 16-year-old who was amazed at how ignorant his father was, and on his twentieth birthday was astounded at how much his father had learned in the last four years. You were probably also enormously grateful for the wise guidance, the caring and supportive relationship, the tolerance shown to your mistakes, to your naivety and need to learn. You might also be remembering how tolerant at times you had to be yourself of attitudes and behaviour that you were sure would never be entertained in your ministry!

Humility and tenacity

All these memories are probably mixed up in varying degrees for you. Thus you are likely to be approaching the responsibility with a mixture of feelings. No matter how many curates have worked with you hitherto, *humility* is the first quality you require and the need for it suddenly looms large on the horizon. After all the Epistle of James warns: 'Not many of you should become teachers, my brothers and sisters, for you know that we who teach will be judged with greater strictness' (3.1). What then is going to help you develop even more your confidence, ideas, and abilities to equip you for the next few years?

In the Anglican Church you will recognize that your incumbency is shared with the bishop – and so obviously is the supervision of a curate. Both of you receive your permission to minister from the bishop; but there is a difference in that you are accountable to the bishop for the personal and ministerial development of your colleague. This is where different dioceses have different patterns and structures. In most dioceses the diocesan bishop shares his oversight with a number of other people: the suffragan bishop (if there is one), the relevant archdeacon, and the officer for ministry and/or the Continuing Ministerial Education (CME) adviser. These latter roles will have slightly different names in different places, but generally the day-today oversight for the curate's training and education will be delegated to a diocesan officer, who for the sake of simplicity in the rest of this book we will refer to as the CME adviser. It will be with him or her that you will have most to do in connection with your junior colleague over the next few years. It is to the CME adviser, in the first instance, that you will need to direct your questions, concerns, worries and need for advice. In fact, in a number of dioceses you will have already had quite a degree of contact with him or her as the diocese seeks to communicate its priorities for training and development and to prepare you for your role. A good working relationship with the officer who is responsible for the oversight of the curate's development in ministry and for your own training and support is obviously crucial to the success of the enterprise.

Another quality that is required is *tenacity*. Being a supervisor will put you under sustained enquiry and the need for reflection. Much that you now take for granted will be examined by the curate. He or she will be keen to know not only why it is like that for you, but also why things are done in such a way in this parish. Curates will also automatically be evaluating the day-to-day life of the parish in the light of what has been learned during initial training. They will continue to make a personal judgement about how all this fits with, or might become part of, their own ministry.

Sometimes incumbents can feel irritated by the constant barrage of enquiry, especially in the early years. Why do you do it like that? Why does this parish not have this? Can you tell me why you handled that meeting like you did? Why are you asking me to do this when you don't want to do it yourself?

Sometimes incumbents feel uncomfortable with being under observation quite so much. Sometimes they feel challenged to think through again the theological, cultural and social reasons for their attitudes, priorities and behaviour. This can be demanding, especially if you are now a little uncertain about why things are as they are! This will be require your time and energy, in an already busy ministry, which leads to the next quality required: *the ability to handle pressure*. Are you able to cope with this? From where will you get your support? In recent experience a group of potential training incumbents formally asked whether supervision could be provided for them as they faced the arrival of a curate in training with them, and in some dioceses it is policy that training incumbents organize supervision for themselves.

Good time management

Incumbents who supervise others will need discipline about their own time management. Have you time to train a curate? Perhaps the better question is, Can you rearrange your priorities so that some things are dropped or postponed for a few years in favour of spending time with a colleague? There is no magic about time management. It is simply a question of priorities and personal organization, and these can be reviewed and learned afresh regularly in ministry, and more is said on this in Chapter 4.

What are you going to give up in order to make quality time for supervising a colleague? If you are going to cope healthily with the pressures and expectations of the next few years as a supervisor a good policy will be to share this question with others in the parish. Thus the parish's expectations of your time and energy stand a chance of being modified in the light of a new situation. This will be important for your sanity.

Some dangerous fantasies need to be debunked. The first is that the arrival of a curate means that ministerial time will increase to 200 per cent of that expected of a single priest. The second is that the 'vicar' can go on doing all he or she has been doing, even if it is recognized that a curate will need to spend time in learning. It is useful advice from the start to begin to encourage the right attitudes among laypeople, which will also make life easier for you. In one diocese potential incumbents were encouraged from the earliest to talk to their parishes about a curate being only part-time, even if she or he was stipendiary. This realism recognizes that the curate will be spending time away from parish ministry on training days, with peer groups, with a tutor, in review conversations with the CME adviser and others, on placements and even short-term secondments, to say nothing of awaydays with the incumbent and other parish staff.

The importance of providing time for supervision with a curate can hardly be overemphasized. Recent experience among CME advisers shows that the most frequent complaint from curates is about not spending enough time with their training incumbents. This concern is supported by the curates' responses to the research questions shown in Table 2.2.

That only just over half the curates in the sample felt they spent enough time in one-to-one conversations with their supervisors is a matter of concern. Curates perceive incumbents as being able to make a distinction between a staff (business) meeting and a supervision

Table 2.2 Curates' views of the time with incumbents

	Agree	?	Disagree
My training incumbent and I did not spend enough time talking together about our ministry	34%	13%	53%

(learning) session. Even so, the number of curates who agreed their incumbents did in fact make this distinction gives no cause for complacency. More will be said about this issue elsewhere in this book.

Self-knowledge

Another quality you will need is *self-knowledge*; such awareness has always been at the heart of Christian discipleship. Four representative figures from different times, different church traditions and different cultures provide evidence of the consistency of this tradition.

Gregory of Nyssa (*c.* CE 330–*c.* 395) wrote: 'Our greatest protection is self-knowledge, and to avoid the delusion that we are seeing ourselves when in reality we are looking at something else.'

And in 1559 John Calvin said:

All the wisdom we possess, that is to say true and sound wisdom, consists of two parts, the knowledge of God and ourselves. But while joined by many bonds which one precedes and brings forth the other is not easy to discern. In the first place no one can look upon himself without immediately turning his thoughts to the contemplation of God in whom he 'lives and moves' (Acts 17.28). (McNeil, 1960)

Clearly for Calvin and Gregory the boundary between the knowledge of God and the knowledge of ourselves is a permeable one. Calvin, perhaps interestingly for a reformation theologian, says access to the knowledge of God can follow directly from knowledge of ourselves.

About the same time and from a different perspective Teresa of Avila, one of the most respected guides in religious development, wrote: 'It is no small pity and shame, that by our own fault, we do not understand ourselves, nor realize who we are . . . knowledge of ourselves is so important.'

In the 1890s Herbert Kelly, founder of the Society of the Sacred Mission and the former Anglican Kelham Theological College, wrote in the *Principles* of the Society: 'There are many things it will not profit you to know, but next to the knowledge of God you are most concerned to know yourself' (Society of the Sacred Mission, XI, 1951).

As well as echoing Calvin this has a surprisingly contemporary ring. Particularly important for you as a training incumbent is to understand your own oversight and management style, and to be able to monitor what effect it has on your inner life. You will need to be flexible and to adapt to the different demands that come from a curate and from a parish. You will need to know yourself well enough and to have the self-confidence to be able to support publicly someone who is working in a different way, and when necessary to address differences in private.

Self-confidence

Self-confidence will be needed by a supervisor since the question of authority is complex in the Church. An incumbent will need to be able to negotiate different sorts of authority with a colleague in different contexts. He or she will need to delegate responsibility for sections of the ministry of the parish and, with it, delegate authority as well. This may mean dealing firmly with 'bypass' when appeals are directed to you over the curate's head. The authority conveyed at ordination to a priest is the same for the newly priested curate as for you, but the authority of oversight in the parish is not. For example, you will expect the curate to contribute to discussions at PCC meetings and offer his or her insights, but what degree of freedom does the curate have to speak at the PCC if he or she wants to disagree with what you have said or to challenge your policies? There is no simple answer except to agree a way of working with the curate.

How will you cope with the natural feelings that may arise when the PCC prefers, perhaps more than once, the options offered by a curate to the established policies that you are known to support? How will you manage yourself when the curate appears to be more popular with some people than you are?

Can you offer a rebuke to the curate, if it is required, in a way that will be acceptable and creative? Does it worry you that this might be necessary?

In the current situation in the Church, a newly ordained person might be more mature in years and with considerably more life experience than an incumbent. If this turns out to be true in your situation how will you think about this?

We have now begun to touch on relationship issues that will be addressed more fully in Chapter 9.

The identification of appropriate training incumbents

Training incumbent proforma

6　Models strategic, reflective, theological thinking in parish leadership;

7　Engages regularly in in-service training and takes time for reading and reflection (Study week?);

8　Takes time for prayer and reflection (Daily Office, Retreats);

9　Is self-aware, secure but not defended, vulnerable but not fragile;

10　Has demonstrated a collaborative approach in discussion, planning and action in the parish;

11　Has been able to let go of responsibility to others, after appropriate training and supervision;

12　Has shared ministry, including difficulties and disappointments, with colleagues;

13　Has a personal theological and spiritual position which is creative and flexible so as to be able to engage and work constructively with different theological and spiritual positions;

14　Has a record of allowing colleagues to develop in ways different from their own;

15　Has an ability to interpret the social dynamics of the parish and to develop a strategy for mission and the implementation of change;

16　Has a genuine desire to be part of the training team rather than wanting an assistant and is therefore willing to agree to enable training experience that makes use of prior experience;

17　Has the ability to help the curate in the process of integrating his/her theological studies with ministerial experience.

Future expectations

18　Will undertake further study to function as a Training Incumbent;

19　Will give time to supervision and planning of training;

20　Is willing to receive supervision in the role of the Training Incumbent;

21　Will invest effort in mobilizing available resources, outside as well as within the parish for the training of a curate;

22　Will give the Initial Ministerial Education, IME, programme a high priority and work in partnership with diocese and Bishop's officers.

Extract from Archbishops' Council (March 2003), Appendix 4.

The extract above is the guidance about the desirable characteristics and qualities to be found in potential training incumbents which has been issued nationally by the Church of England. Further information about nationally provided guidelines for training incumbents in the skills for effective supervision is to be found in Appendix 9.

Although the next chapter is beginning to be anticipated, it is clear from this guidance that encouraging learning only by watching and copying, or helping a curate by trying to produce a clone of yourself, are not appropriate models for supervision.

This chapter has explored the skills and qualities that should be demonstrated, or acquired, by those who are asked to supervise curates. The next chapter describes the important developments in adult education theory and practice and their relevance for supervisors of newly ordained women and men.

Points for reflection

- How well do you fit the profile indicated by the items in the boxed list above? Could you rate yourself on a 1 (low) to 5 (high) scale for each of the items above? (If you do so perhaps you could also ask someone who knows you well or, better still, works with you to rate you. Comparing the two sets of answers could offer you insight and aid your self-knowledge. It could be helpful to talk the findings over with your work consultant or spiritual director.)
- How do you feel now about taking on the supervision of a curate?
- Who or what has helped you to self-knowledge – perhaps a spiritual director, critical friend, supervisor or a ministerial review?
- How good are you at using the insights you gain?
- Can you access your feelings, and can you get a sense of what belongs to you, what belongs to the role, and what comes from elsewhere?
- Can you set aside the time sufficiently often for supervision with your colleague? With whom will you talk through this issue concerning time?
- Are you able to make it clear in the parish what work you are dropping or postponing while you have a curate in post?

3

Helping people learn

- What was the last thing you learned about ministry?
- How did you learn it? Were you told something? Did you read it somewhere? Was it the result of a discussion? Did you watch someone else? Maybe you just thought, 'If I did this it could be better.' Did you experiment and try something different?
- How prominent is teaching within your ministry? Who do you teach? And do you teach formally or more informally? Is preaching part of your teaching ministry?
- How would you describe to someone else the differences between helping children learn and helping adults learn?

In the previous chapter we looked at the qualities and skills required of supervisors, and the specific qualities desirable by those of curates. In this chapter we turn to that aspect of supervision which is more focused into the quadrant of the model that is about learning and teaching.

We begin with some general ideas about how adults learn before applying them specifically to the supervision of a curate and of others. How did you answer the last question above – about the difference between children and adults? If you identified at least the two key differences – that children don't often know what they need to learn, and that adults do; and that children would find it difficult to assess how much they know, while adults are often well aware of the gaps (and of how to fill them) – then you already know a lot about how adults learn.

Adult education in theory and practice has grown enormously in the last 40 years and is now a sophisticated professional discipline in its own right. Many years ago tutors in the various community-based adult education programmes (e.g. those offered by the Workers Educational Association) were aware of the difference between lecturing to younger undergraduates and teaching older people in the community who signed up for classes out of interest. Adults in the community always brought with them life experience, which they related to the concepts and theories to which they were being introduced. They were highly motivated and very curious. They had to be taught differently – with much more interaction, discussion and plenty of room for questions. The tutors found people were keen to contribute their own ideas. The Open University has provided an impetus, and brought great experience to this growth industry.

We begin with some key thinkers in the field and their seminal ideas. The first of these is Malcolm Knowles (1984). He drew attention to some assumptions about adults. First, adults are independent and self-directing. Second, adults have accumulated a pool of experience that can be a rich resource for learning. Third, adults value learning that is directly related to everyday life and work. Fourth, adults are more interested in problem-based methods of learning than in theoretical approaches. Fifth, it is assumed that adults are motivated more by internal motivators than external rewards.

In Chapter 1 we noted the problems created for the Church in living in a rapidly changing, technological and consumer-based society. The eternal values to which we subscribe and which we wish to promote have to be recast for each generation if they are to be understood as related to the life experience of our contemporaries. It is not just a question of devising new methods, of learning about PowerPoint; it is a question of language and translation, and even of phrasing the things of God within new concepts. All of this will be familiar to the clergy of today's Church – it serves to point to the ever more pressing need for continued learning in professional ministry. A number of reports, books, handbooks and policy publications have appeared in the last 20 years to help us cope with this. A list of useful titles is given in the Further Reading section at the end of this book. The *Alpha* and *Emmaus* courses are examples of how many of Knowles's ideas have been incorporated into common practice. Contrast the methods used by the *Emmaus* programme(s) with how things were done in the Church years ago.

Another important thinker was Candy (1991) who developed Knowles's ideas further. He identified a large number of abilities associated with adult learning. The key skills are the ability to be methodical and disciplined, the skill of logical and analytical thinking, the ability to be both collaborative and also independent, the ability to be both open and curious, and the abilities to be creative, reflective and self-aware. Adult learners need the opportunity to develop and practise these skills. If given these opportunities learners will ask questions, critically appraise new information and identify their own knowledge and the gaps in their learning; and most importantly they will be able to reflect critically on their own learning process and its outcomes. Tight (1983) highlighted the need to see adult learners as partners in the enterprise rather than recipients of others' decisions.

Albert Bandura (1986) also made an important contribution to the debate. He drew attention to adults' judgement of their own competence in different situations. He claimed that this is central to their performance. Learners' performance is dependent on judgements such as: how they decide to act, how much effort they invest in the activities, how long they persist in the face of adversity, and whether their approach to the task is characterized by assurance or anxiety. The judgements an individual makes may or may not be accurate but they are based on four main sources of information: performance attainments, observations of other people, verbal persuasion and physiological state. Thus sometimes the fact that other people perform tasks successfully can strengthen adults' belief that they can perform similar tasks, especially when the tasks are unfamiliar. However, this depends on self-confidence.

Enabling people to learn by experience, and then to reflect on that experience, depends on the self-confidence they possess. For example, some adults lead intercessions in public worship. The prayer offered on behalf of all can be sensitive, informed and far-reaching. It can be more effective than those of the clergy. But often laity fail more in confidence than in competence when it comes to leading intercessions. Paulo Freire (1970) has long been influential in education in the Church, both formal and informal. He showed that people can think for themselves, decide what is important and decide what action to take through effective facilitation as much as they can by traditional teaching. He particularly emphasized the maximization of learning that is achieved in small groups.

The last of our seminal theorists is Donald Schön (1987) who identified two types of theory that are used by professionals. He called them the *espoused theory* and the *theory in use*. Put very simply, *espoused theory* is what you say you do and why you do it, and *theory in use* is what you actually do and the reasons that can be deduced from your actions. He showed that the espoused theory does not and cannot guide practice. It is the theory in use that is more reliable when adults seek to resolve problems. For example there may be a difference between what clergy were taught and believe about baptism (the espoused theory) and practical parish policies concerning the public baptism of infants. Some people may think it highly desirable that baptisms should take place at the Parish Communion on

Sunday mornings (the espoused theory), but the reality of parish life and pastoral politics could make it necessary to conduct baptisms with groups of families on Sunday afternoons (theory in use). Schön would not say one 'theory' is right and the other wrong, or that compromise is always a good thing. He just draws attention to the difference between what we think and what we do – and says that what we do is the best guide to the solutions professionals employ. Understanding the distinctions between the two approaches could help to avoid conflict between incumbents and curates and an internal conflict for the curate as he or she wrestles with competing ideas.

Yet even theories in use tend to be provisional, since real-life problems present themselves as incomplete, partially understood, and in complex situations. In this case, the concern of the professional learner has to be the discovery of the right questions to be asked or resolved rather than a body of knowledge, rules, principles or agreed procedures that are more easily understood. It is in this situation that reflection is so crucial. Therefore the ability to promote reflection is fundamental among the skills of supervision. Before we turn to reflection let us apply these theories to helping curates to learn, and see what practical guidance they offer.

The contributions of these thinkers have been accepted into initial learning in most professions, including training for ministry. Curates will arrive with experience of this sort of educational process having studied on ministerial training courses and at theological colleges and these principles will be fundamental to the process of supervision.

Helping curates learn

First a brief summary of the main points:

- Adult learners need a climate that allows people to feel safe and comfortable about expressing themselves.
- Adult learners should be involved in planning the methods and the content of the learning.
- Adult learners should be involved in identifying their own needs to develop internal motivation.
- Adult learners should be allowed to formulate their own learning objectives to give them more control.
- Adult learners should be encouraged to identify resources and devise strategies for achieving their objectives.

- Adult learners need support and encouragement from peers and teachers in carrying out their plans.
- Finally, adult learners need to be involved in evaluating their own learning – and this helps to develop the skills of critical reflection that are discussed in the next section of this chapter.

This list implies a high degree of self-direction on the part of adult learners. How does this apply to curates?

The first thing to note in this summary is that motivation is rarely the problem. In our experience curates are only too keen to learn, to put into practice the learning acquired before ordination, to try out the ideas they have been thinking about, and to become experienced, effective and competent priests of the Church.

If curates are to feel safe in taking risks, trying things out, making mistakes and learning from them, then they need an accepting, risk-taking and forgiving environment. In this the most important relationship is that with you, the supervising incumbent. Your curate will look to you for the knowledge of how things are done, when and in what style. They will want to try out their own ideas, and look to you for permission, support and a critique. They will expect to be accepted unconditionally by you – and also to be corrected at times.

Curates also want to be guided into the mores of public ministry. They will want others to recognize them by their behaviour as competent priests of the Church – and to be trustworthy as such. This is where you will offer guidance, formally through instruction on how things are done, e.g. what is good practice at a crematorium or what the diocesan process of approving churchyard memorials is. You will also offer guidance, through modelling, on the behaviour and attitudes consistent with good pastoral ministry. In this way, both consciously and unconsciously you will be helping the curate to be an effective professional in ministry; and you will also in turn help them to model to others those gifts of the spirit that Paul lists in Ephesians: love, joy, peace, goodness, patience, kindness, faithfulness, gentleness, self-control, etc.

This is an awesome responsibility, for we spend a lot of our subsequent ministry reacting against or developing what we experienced with our first incumbent. Training incumbents and curates work together in a complex and intimate relationship, at times not unlike that of marriage with its shared knowledge of each other, its trust and even affection, and its struggle with finding the right balance between autonomy as an individual priest and interdependence as one of the ministerial leadership team in the parish. It was not for nothing that we suggested the first requirement of potential training incumbents is humility. A good working relationship is crucial – without it there will be little training and little learning. One curate wrote of her experience:

> ... because I had such a good relationship with my training incumbent, my curacy worked, and not because he was necessarily a good model incumbent. As a trainer he wasn't great, but his ability to boost my confidence and sense of security and belonging enabled me to grow and develop. By him, and importantly, by the congregation, I was 'loved' into the role and I shall always be grateful for that.

This woman is clearly describing a safe environment in which to learn, whatever else might have been lacking.

We noted next in the summary above that curates will learn best if they are allowed to formulate their own learning objectives to give them more control. Deciding what you need to learn not only enhances your motivation and commitment, it also enables you to review your experience and identify more clearly what you already know. However there is a balance to be struck.

Those being ordained don't always know what they don't know – and you will be aware of their need to know certain things about ordained ministry in the parish. For example, newly ordained men and women may not know about the diocesan policy on ministry leadership teams and how these are adapted to suit local conditions, traditions and experience. Without this knowledge curates may make inappropriate assumptions about how they are to relate to lay leaders. Also no training incumbent would want a curate to make a mess of a pastoral interaction for lack of knowledge about the parish's attitude to the remarriage of divorced people. At the same time there are all the legal requirements to do with marriage forms and diocesan returns and fees, all of which are matters clergy in their post of first responsibility find difficult if nobody has taken time to teach them in their curacy. There is a balance to be struck between giving essential information and allowing people to learn by making mistakes. The balance is derived from your overall care for the curate and other people. Here of course is where your wisdom and greater experience will guide the managerial element within your overall supervision.

There is also a balance to be struck between requiring that the curate knows certain things and allowing them to set their own learning objectives. Occasionally, for the sake of the curate, some things have to be said and then a supervisor will need a robust self-confidence. A curate was uncomfortable wearing vestments and was keen to get out of them as soon as possible after the service. The training incumbent's response was to say, 'You will wear vestments in this parish because it is our custom, and also until it ceases to be an issue for you; until that moment arrives it will be a distraction.' She was not only being honest in the moment, but giving wise direction at a critical time.

The next point from our summary is about adult learners needing support and encouragement from peers and teachers in carrying out their plans. Curates will also be more committed to their learning goals if they are encouraged to identify resources and devise strategies for achieving their objectives. It could be more useful for a supervisor to ask, 'Where do you think you might look for the answers?' than to offer the curate either the incumbent's answers, or to suggest a method or source of exploration. Wise incumbents will often wait until they are asked for their opinion – not always easy in the pressure of busy parish life – but this is much more effective. Guiding the curate in devising a strategy and suggesting a number of people to talk to is obviously helpful, but supervisors need to be aware of their own desire to help, and to give it a back seat while encouraging the curate to develop their own ideas.

The curate can then plan what she or he needs to learn, in what order and at what speed. The supervising incumbent will then want to ask follow-up questions that check on progress and monitor that the curate is still on track. How are you getting on with . . . ? What have you discovered about . . . ? These are questions that offer support and encouragement and imply that you have a real interest and desire to help.

The last point in our summary is about the need for the curate to be involved in evaluating his or her own learning. In this way the individual can decide how much they have learned and how well they have learned it. They can identify what questions remain, and when

Good advice for supervisors from a theologian

The fatal pedagogical error is to throw answers like stones at the heads of those who have not yet asked questions.

Attributed to Paul Tillich.

their learning about a particular topic is complete. The experience of the Open University is that adults are nearly always more rigorous in assessing their own work than tutors. Curates who are treated as adults can be trusted. At times your involvement in assessment may need to be no more than that of offering praise and encouragement, and valuing the achievement. At other times a rigorous critique will be required or requested.

What questions will help?

Chapter 6 emphasizes, in connection with aiding reflection, that one of the fundamental skills of the supervisor is the ability to ask the right kind of question at the right time. Geoff Maughan, in an article published in the *British Journal of Theological Education*, 'Asking Questions Afterwards' (2004), looks at the conversation between the rich young man and Jesus recorded in Mark 10.17–31. Based on the idea of Stephen Pattison of a 'critical conversation', Maughan explores the biblical basis for asking questions and the example of Jesus as both a teacher and an enquirer. This idea of the critical conversation is echoed in Mark 8.14–21 when, after the feeding of the four thousand, Jesus asks his disciples nine questions.

The basic skill for supervisors is asking open questions rather than questions which can be answered by yes or no. You may find the following sequence of questions as helpful as we have, in supporting self-directed learning:

- What did you set out to achieve?
- What problems did you encounter?
- How did you overcome them?
- How satisfied are you with the results?
- What questions are you left with?

Other questions can of course be added, for example:

- What theological sense do you make of this?
- How does this connect with your initial learning for ministry?

Guiding your colleague through a set of questions like this helps them to gain an overall appreciation of their learning; to express it and own it, and to gain confidence in their ability to devise a process for tackling something else. You will also signal that you are genuinely interested in the curate's development, and not just in another pair of hands to help in the parish. The overall message is to treat your curate as an adult who is highly motivated, very committed, self-directed and self-organizing.

This may seem trite and fairly obvious. However, there is evidence of inadequate supervision provided by some incumbents. A curate wrote: 'Supervision was an unplanned informal chat about an issue in the vestry after the service.' Another said: 'I am relieved to be serving only a two-year curacy and have found this period disempowering rather than building up. I look forward to regaining confidence in a new post.' There is other evidence of patronizing and domineering attitudes on the part of incumbents in Neil Burgess's *Into Deep Water* (1998).

It is also worth saying that there is evidence of very good practice:

> He assumed I would work in the same way as him. As we got to know each other more his expectations of me reflected my personality. He didn't change how he did things – but he didn't expect me to do the same as him any longer.

This chapter has offered some principles that underpin good practice in helping adults to learn. The main points of relevance for church life have been summarized and placed in the context of supervising a curate. Before reflection in detail is examined in Chapter 6, working with difference is the subject of the next two chapters.

Points for reflection

- Go back to the questions given at the start of this chapter and have another look at them below. Would your answers be any different now?
- What was the last thing you learned about ministry?
- How did you learn it? Were you told something? Did you read it somewhere? Was it the result of a discussion? Did you watch someone else? Maybe you just thought, 'If I did this it could be better.' Did you experiment and try something different?
- How prominent is teaching within your ministry? Who do you teach? And do you teach formally or more informally? Is preaching part of your teaching ministry?
- How would you describe to someone else the differences between helping children learn and helping adults learn?
- Have you learned anything by looking at these questions again?

4

Working with difference

- How do you regard differences between people in ministry?
- Do you feel more comfortable having as much in common as possible and do you feel this makes it easier to make decisions and work together?
- Do you feel more comfortable with varieties of experience, attitude and beliefs and think that this makes ministry richer . . . or what?
- How much did you have in common with those who have supervised you; did you choose them because of similarity or because of difference?

In the previous chapter we explored the theories and practice of adult education as they apply to the supervision of curates. We saw what helps and what hinders the learning of a curate as he or she takes up a public ministry with people and in society. In this chapter the range of differences that might exist between the supervisor and the person supervised is considered and how those differences affect the working relationship and the way supervision is experienced by each. This chapter will look at personal differences that we do not choose such as gender and age, and those that we do such as theological stance and lifestyle. In particular two models of difference that arise from ideas and theories, e.g. psychological differences and differences of learning styles, are dealt with in some depth.

A working group from the Ministry Division of the Church of England has identified skills for training incumbents as ability to:

- listen
- own one's own feelings
- be open to different lifestyles and ways of working
- create a helping relationship
- ask open questions and to be genuinely curious
- be sensitive to where the curate is 'at'
- wait for the curate's growth and development
- recognize the significance of the curate's resistance
- acknowledge and use the process going on with supervision

- share the agenda-setting for supervision
- believe that mistakes are valuable.

Many of these qualities highlight the importance of understanding and working with difference. Some of the obvious things that make us different from one another open the discussion, starting with those we might think we can choose and change and then moving to those differences about which we can do nothing. Not only is previous experience of supervision significant; our personal and professional histories have a profound effect on the supervisory relationship.

Ministerial differences – theology and church tradition

The differences most often remarked on by curates are the different understandings of ministry and working styles between them and their training incumbents. The calling to public ministry stands within a long and noble tradition often explained in the language of sacrifice and expressed in extremely long working hours. While the day off and the use of the answer-phone have become accepted by most clergy, working weeks of 60 to 70 hours are often the norm. Making time for family, friends and hobbies is often thought of as an indulgence in the light of the demands and needs of the world and the call of Christ.

The culture of modern theological education and ministerial formation before ordination in our colleges, courses and schemes tends to emphasize the importance of caring for oneself, taking adequate time off and time for family, and finding a healthy work–life balance. Associated with this new culture is the ability to say no. That is not to say that many new curates find this an easy culture to develop. As a matter of fact some find the more traditional culture of their supervising incumbent quite attractive; others find themselves drawn into it against their better judgement. Even so, some work hard at maintaining the balance and often feel at odds with their training incumbent.

These differences of style and working culture lie at the heart of many of the problems faced in the supervisory relationship and they need to be explored and talked about often. In one relationship this clash of cultures led the training incumbent to write about his deacon that he was not sure she was ready to take up the demands of their priestly calling. The same curate complained that her future was being undermined by a vicar who completely overworked and had a family whose lifestyle was wholly dedicated to enabling him to work all the hours there are, and was quite different from the curate's own.

It is very important to explore these differences and talk about them all the time, and to dig a bit below the surface. For we all know that we do not always practise what we preach, nor do we own up to those behaviours which we know are part and parcel of our ministry but of which we do not really approve. CME officers never cease to be surprised at how many working clergy claim to have time off and work reasonable hours, but in reality don't.

Theological attitudes and church tradition backgrounds are also potential areas of conflict and are likely to have featured in the initial contact and interview between curate and incumbent. A church tradition in the receiving parish which is felt to be congenial to the curate is an important consideration in matching curates and incumbents. It is also necessary for incumbents interviewing prospective curates to be aware that most curates feel a pressure to accept the first parish that they view. Ordinands are nearly always anxious about being 'left behind' or being seen as difficult to place, or even of feeling after considering a parish, 'This will do.' They often settle for compromise. Sometimes people can mean quite different things when they indicate that they are evangelical or catholic or liberal, and it is always worth testing what is meant with some con-crete examples, for instance talking about baptism policy, the remar-riage of divorcees, evangelism strategies, attitudes to gay and lesbian people, headship of women, the values of modern and traditional church music, or allowing a yoga class to use the church hall. All these can illuminate nuances of difference which can escalate into serious conflict or frustration with very little provocation.

Sometimes an incumbent will think that it will be really helpful for the parish to experience the ministry of someone of a different tradition from their own. It may be thought that for a three-year curacy this can bring new life and discipleship. Sometimes a curate will look for a parish of a different tradition from their own upbringing or training because they think it will enrich their learning and for-mation. Either way this is a fine idea; but it needs to be talked about carefully. If this sort of difference can be embraced then it works, but if difference is perceived to be disloyalty, or even of signs pointing to sinful discipleship or a deeply flawed ministry, then it is difficult to see how a working relationship can be sustained.

Table 4.1 Fulfilment of curates' expectations of the title parish

	Agree	*?*	*Disagree*
My training in my title parish prepared me very well for ordained ministry	74%	18%	8%
My training in my title parish took account of my individual gifts and needs	69%	10%	21%
My training in my title parish was reasonably satisfactory overall	75%	7%	18%
My training in my title parish matched my initial expectations	60%	8%	32%
Reflecting on my experience I think more thought should be given to where curates are placed	61%	19%	19%

The question of whether parishes come up to curates' expectations is illuminated by research findings (Tilley, 2006). These suggest that for many curates an adjustment takes place between expectations and reality.

Table 4.1 indicates that on the whole the curates in the research sample appear to be a relatively contented group. Either their expectations might be thought to have been largely fulfilled, or they adapted relatively easily to a situation which was rather different from what they expected before ordination. Nevertheless, 61 per cent considered that more thought should be given to where curates are placed. This might be thought to contrast with the higher figure for satisfaction overall. This apparent difference might be explained by personal adjustment to a situation different from that expected – 'It wasn't what I wanted, but we got along OK, and I made the best of it, and it turned out all right.'

Nevertheless, as the curate enters public ministry it is likely that there will be more than one occasion that will result in difference, or even conflict, on the basis of values and theology. The sine qua non of resolution is to talk about it together, as early as possible. A sharing of spiritual, vocational and educational stories that have been influential in each person will take the heat out of a situation which could be frustrating for all, and will create understanding. We would emphasize the necessity of both supervisor and supervised engaging openly in telling the stories which have formed their stance or attitude. This is not just an issue for the curate.

There are few theological differences which cannot be creatively accepted if each point of view is heard in a steady relationship of mutual trust and openness. It is the responsibility of the incumbent to give the necessary information on parish policy and values, not of the curate to ask since he or she may not be fully aware of all the policies which may be important to the local church.

Age

Is age a factor in supervision? At first sight you may respond, 'Is age important?' But reflection will show that a notable difference in age between incumbent and curate could be significant.

It is more likely than at any time previously that an incumbent could be noticeably younger than a curate. This will be more to be expected in the case of volunteer and part-time (non-stipendiary and ordained local) curates. These ministers are more likely to be offering for public ministry in the last quarter of life, perhaps after a previous career.

The younger incumbent will be wise if she or he recognizes that longer experience in ordained ministry is not the same as maturity in the experience of life. There will be occasions when a younger incumbent will need to listen to the different wisdom offered by an older curate even if the curate has been ordained only recently. It is the possibility of this difference in age which makes supervision in public ministry different from that often experienced in other helping professions.

But apart from any discrepancy between the ages of incumbent and curate, is the age of the curate significant in its own right?

There is research evidence that points to the possibility that incumbents respond to older curates differently from younger curates. The findings indicate that incumbents (of any age) are more likely to treat older curates with a degree of tolerance and laxity than younger curates; and they are more likely to expect younger curates to be more ordered and systematic than they expect older curates to be.

Older curates were significantly more likely than younger curates to report that their incumbents expected them to work flexibly and spontaneously and not to be upset by last-minute changes (Tilley, 2006).

Younger curates were significantly more likely than older curates to report that they were expected to list and order tasks to be done, to be punctual and to give their incumbents plenty of notice of agreed plans (Tilley, 2006).

It may not be a great surprise after all, but it is clear that age is a significant factor in the supervisory relationship and appears to influence incumbents' expectations of curates. Potential incumbents of curates may need to check that the expectations they have are appropriate for the individual man or woman placed with them, and the only way to do this is by open discussion.

We turn now to differences in the supervisory relationship that result from chosen lifestyles.

Singleness, married and partnership relationships

Research findings show that a large proportion of curates feel their incumbents are sensitive to the needs of married curates, of those with young families and of single people. Table 4.2 offers the evidence for this.

We have already drawn attention to differences in approach to working style and method and these are often acted out in attitudes to family and singleness. Married curates and those in committed relationships will need to protect time for the partner especially where the partner works what we might call normal office hours. The curate may feel squeezed between the Charybdis of time with the partner and the Scylla of time for parishioners in evenings and at weekends. This dilemma may be a novel experience for the newly ordained and while incumbents may have developed ways of

Table 4.2 Curates' views of help with managing time and priorities

	Agree	*?*	*Disagree*
In my partnership with my training incumbent he/she took my personal circumstances – e.g. married, single, divorced, etc. – into account	85%	6%	9%
My training incumbent enabled me to develop an ability to balance competing claims on my time for family, friends and ministry	65%	11%	24%
My training incumbent enabled me to develop the ability to respond appropriately to personal stress and strain	52%	26%	22%

working as a result of long experience, curates may need support lest the natural enthusiasm for ministry makes intemperate demands on social, domestic and other commitments. Similarly single curates need to protect time for friends (who may be living at a distance), and for friendships that may lead to intimate partnerships. Other questions of whether incumbents model good practice and also help curates with managing pressure and time are dealt with later in this chapter.

One of the communication issues highlighted by one curate is the role of the incumbent's spouse. Where that spouse is active in the Church and even in leadership the curate could experience difficulties in obtaining information she or he needs from the incumbent. This situation might just result from carelessness, where the 'staff meeting' takes place over the breakfast table, or as a result of the incumbent having talked through what he/she needed to do already and therefore energy for communicating with the curate, whose experience and knowledge is trusted less, is diminished. Particular care needs to be taken when both incumbent and spouse are ordained. Similar situations might arise where both a curate and spouse are ordained, but they are likely to be less important because of the relative influence and power held by the incumbent.

Choices about busyness, priorities and time management

What incumbents choose to model, consciously or unconsciously, for the newly ordained and how they help them cope with competing priorities is the focus here. We start by looking at whether curates perceived incumbents as helping them in this area.

Table 4.2 offers research evidence that curates did not regard incumbents as being very helpful to them over managing competing time priorities. There may be a number of reasons for this. One reason could be that incumbents were not good at managing these time pressures for themselves. There is a story about the doctor who said she had visited many men on their deathbeds, but never yet heard any who said they wished they had spent more time at work.

The first item in Table 4.2 sought curates' opinions about whether their incumbents took into account their personal situation. For example it might be thought that a curate with a family might need to spend time with children in the early evening to help with homework or with bedtime. A single curate would need a different sort of flexibility if she or he is to maintain contact with friends and avoid loneliness. Although phrased in generalities, the item created opportunity for the respondents to reflect any felt dissatisfactions in their personal, as opposed to ministerial, relationships. It is good to report that the great majority (85 per cent) of curates felt their incumbents did in fact take their personal situation into account. This is rather different from the findings reported by Burgess (1998) and suggests that the clergy in the Church of England at least are getting better at this aspect of supervision.

A rather lower percentage (65 per cent) said that their incumbents had actually helped them to prioritize their time. This may be because either the curates did not reveal any problems about managing time, or incumbents did not perceive it. This lower reported satisfaction could also be a function of the incumbents' inability to manage their own time effectively.

A much lower percentage (52 per cent) felt that their incumbents helped them make an appropriate response to strain and stress. This finding might conceal a failure on the part of curates themselves to recognize or a willingness to acknowledge any strain and stress. This finding raises questions about how men and women are preparing for the likely greater pressures of a second post, when they will be under less supervision and more dependent on their own inner resources and habits of discipline. A failure to nurture their humanity and personhood in healthy relationships can lead to the stress of professional interactions becoming excessive (Irvine, 1997, and especially chapter 6). Acquiring good time management is a skill which is best learnt early in ministry. Archbishop Rowan Williams, in an address to celebrate the centenary of Ripon Theological College, Cuddesdon, laid great emphasis on the space and freedom to be a discerning interpreter on behalf of the community: 'The priest has to have the opportunity of not being so swamped with "duties" that he or she can't maintain a sense of the whole landscape' (Williams, 2004). That opportunity is at risk where there is not only stress and strain but poor time management.

It seems clear that a difference of approximately 33 per cent between agreement on the majority of responses to first and last items in Table 4.2 indicates that most incumbents were able to cope with the facts of their curate's personal situation but were less likely proactively to help with managing competing claims as the curate adjusted to a new role and its demands. Perhaps the incumbents themselves were poor managers of competing claims on their own time and not skilled at setting priorities for themselves. The danger of a perpetuating cycle of dysfunction among self-managing and self-directing ministers is apparent. This raises important questions about the need to identify potential incumbents who demonstrate an ability to manage their time, priorities and the expectations of their ministry effectively.

Nevertheless, the findings show that just over half of the research curates were able to say that they had been enabled by their incumbents to deal with personal stress and strain. For these curates the future might be thought to appear brighter than for the others.

Some differences between supervisors and supervised that arise from choices have been examined; we now turn to those differences that are not chosen. Some of these 'givens', e.g. race and gender, will be obvious at the interview; others, such as sexual orientation, may not be easily perceived.

Race and gender

We bring to the calling of ministry and to the supervisory relationship the body with which we were born, and with which among other things we have become very familiar, with its gender, colour and sexual orientation. These personal aspects, the families in which we grew up, and the social contexts in which we learned about life, all help to shape who we are, how we feel about ourselves, and the perspectives through which we see others and the world around us.

These issues concern the feelings about how we are perceived by others, and their attitudes and behaviour towards us. Race and gender are not no-go areas in supervision. A black curate in an urban priority area (UPA) parish in a Midlands city began his ministry journal reflecting on what it felt like to walk around the 'white highlands' on the morning after ordination wearing a dog collar. His incumbent had much experience of working-class parishes and she was understanding and supportive in what was sometimes a challenging environment for his ministry.

Sometimes gender and/or race can be issues between an incumbent and curate. Neil Burgess quotes some bad experiences of women being supervised by men. One woman illustrates their concerns by describing how she felt patronized by her incumbent, '... somehow it's like you are my father, and I don't want that ...' (Burgess, 1998). A female NSM felt her incumbent's attitude to women was inappropriate; nevertheless she said, 'I have felt it to be part of my loyalty to my training incumbent to protect him and the parish from my real feelings' (Tilley, 2006). It is sad that this latter couple were not able to talk openly over the issue of gender and move to a creative, trusting and mutually respectful relationship.

Ignoring the issue and feelings that differences of gender and/or race arouse in us will run the risk of an explosion in the relationship or its deterioration to the point of disintegration. If these differences are not acknowledged, and their impact discussed openly at the start of the supervisory relationship, they could become much more difficult to deal with later. If either party becomes concerned or apprehensive about the attitudes or behaviour of the other and finds it difficult to name the worries openly, the only avenue open is to discuss the issues elsewhere. The nettle has to be grasped without blame. As the incumbent and curate work together and get to know each other their contract may need to be renegotiated. The best way to do this is to build a review into the contract every few months so that the relationship between supervisor and supervisee is examined. But we are anticipating detailed advice offered in Chapter 10.

Sexual orientation

The question about different sexual orientations is, at the time of writing, one about which the Church has chosen to fight! This may make it even more problematic in supervision. What makes it one of the most difficult personal differences to consider is the way sexual orientation is related to culture, theology, tradition, morality and views of humanity. These come together in a very thick soup that many people find indigestible.

A heterosexual incumbent discovering (or perhaps suspecting) that a curate is gay or lesbian might want to offer support, but needs to do so in a very sensitive way. The incumbent does not have the right to probe, which may threaten the curate's privacy. A situation like this is potentially painful for both, apart from any contrasting theological attitudes that may be held. Homophobia and inherent heterosexism in society and the Church mean that anything the incumbent does in this area is risk-taking. Even if the issue is not a personal concern of the supervisor, discrimination generally means that it is a potential problem for the gay or lesbian curate.

Whatever the curate decides to do – whether to come out or not – he or she will need considerable understanding and support from the incumbent. A lesbian social worker quoted in Brown and

Bourne (1996) said that the decision as to whether to come out or not to her supervisor 'felt like jumping off a cliff'; it could feel no less risky for someone who is ordained.

All of these individual differences will feed into the awareness and expectations you hold of your curate, and also of her or his expectations of you. They may not all be problematical, and it would be a counsel of perfection and undesirable to say that they must all be discussed openly at interview. But incumbents may want to ask which individual differences really matter to them, and whether these should be raised initially when considering a potential curate. The differences are important because they will affect the working relationship and how supervision will be conducted and experienced. Awareness is at least half of the solution to minimizing difficulties.

So, what to do about differences that come to light? Exploring your differences once you start working together might well feel a bit risky. However at the start we can assume optimism and goodwill in both partners. Looking at differences in a relationship of mutual trust and respect is likely to lead to greater understanding, increased creativity and less conflict. We offer in the example below a structured way to do this. The earlier this exercise is attempted the greater will be the benefit to the developing relationship. If it is left until a problem arises it will be more difficult and could be seen by the other as manipulative, or as a way of managing a crisis about one difference, which will limit the effectiveness of the exercise.

EXAMPLE 4.1 **An exercise to do with your curate or a person you supervise**

1 Write down all your similarities and differences. Both of you do it separately.
2 Each person draws up two lists. On one list record all the areas where you experience similarities. On the other list all the areas where you experience differences between you.
3 Now sit down together and compare first your lists of similarities. Notice the areas you have both included; find more similarities together. Feel good about this and encourage each other. This is very important in enabling you to discuss your differences without reacting negatively.

4 Explain and discuss your differences. Read them aloud to each other. For each item explain the attitudes, thoughts and feelings which underlie it.

5 Classify and order your differences. Take one list at a time and indicate how you feel about each one using the symbols:

☺ 'I am happy about this difference. The difference is OK. Let's have more of it.'

☹ 'I have difficulty accepting this difference. You are OK, but I experience this as not-OK. I would like you to change your behaviour if you want to.'

☺ 'I do not have any strong feelings about this difference. I accept it and can live with it.'

6 Make an agreement. Discuss the assessments in detail. Ignore the neutral ones. Be open towards each other's negative assessments and see them as a challenge to improve. Make a contract to specify in which areas you are prepared to follow the other's desire for change; in which areas each of you is not prepared to change; in which areas you accept that the other person is not going to change after having heard the reasons for his or her behaviour or attitudes.

The way personal differences affect the attitudes and assumptions both supervisor and supervised hold about each other has been the focus of this chapter. The next chapter looks at two important ways of organizing our differences that are highly relevant for supervision in ministry.

Points for reflection

• What differences could get in the way of your ability to offer supervision?
• What differences make the experience creative for both of you?
• Do you feel more or less confident about working with difference than you did when you started this chapter?

5

Models of difference

- Are you familiar with the concept of psychological type?
- Do you know what your Myers–Briggs type is?
- How familiar are you with adult learning styles?
- Do you have a view about whether you are an activist, reflector, theorist or pragmatist when it comes to your own learning?
- Can you answer these questions for those you supervise?

In the previous chapter we invited you to consider the range of differences that might exist between you and the person you supervise, and to think about how those differences affect your working relationship and the way you supervise. This chapter will look at two models that arise from ideas that try to interpret human differences and similarities.

Some people appear to be shy and prefer others to initiate a conversation, while other people are happy to take the initiative and seem to do so naturally. Some people are uncomfortable and feel constrained with too much tidiness about them and others feel comfortably relaxed when there is order and neatness and know instantly where to find things.

We shall look at two models which have been offered to help us understand some of the differences and similarities. These help us to value difference and appreciate the gifts of others. The first one is the model of psychological type derived from Carl Jung known as the Myers–Briggs Type Indicator™ (MBTI). You may be familiar with the MBTI or have heard of it because many people in the churches find it a useful and popular way of looking at human nature.

The second idea was proposed by Kolb and concerns how we learn. We shall be looking also at the Honey and Mumford model of adult learning styles. This is also popular in church circles. It illuminates the different ways in which adults prefer to learn and it is frequently used in centres of initial training for ministry. In some dioceses it is also used with training incumbents and curates.

Psychological type is a good place to begin. If you are familiar with the MBTI model and its questionnaire you may wish to skip the next three sections and continue with the section that relates type preferences to the supervisory relationship on page 48.

Models of personality

We begin by placing the MBTI in context so that it is clear what is being claimed for it and what is not. There are a number of theories of human personality. Over the centuries, from Plato to the present day, various thinkers have attempted to distinguish and categorize human temperament and character. Some recent theories have made use of either a test or an inventory questionnaire that attempts to discover human characteristics objectively. All theories have two aims in common. First, they attempt to discover categories of people; for example extraverts, neurotics, depressives. Second, they attempt to explain differences between people; for example he is more aggressive than she; she makes decisions in a different way from him. All theories of personality tend to attract their supporters and critics.

Jung's psychological typology

Carl Jung considered whether people can be categorized as types. This is the approach on which theory the MBTI is based. Carl Jung locates a psychology of consciousness within his overall scheme of opposed psychological factors. The ideas summarized here are reported in *Psychological Types* (Jung, 1971, first published in English in 1923).

The first of the oppositions is introversion and extraversion, the two preferences that belong to the inner and the outer worlds. Extraverts are people whose interest is attracted to the outer world of people and things. They draw energy from their engagement with the outer world and tend to be more easily exhausted by activity in the inner world than introverts. Introverts are people whose interest is oriented in the opposite direction, to the inner world. Introverts are attracted to the inner world of concepts, memories and ideas. They draw energy from within themselves and tend to be more easily exhausted by activity in the outer world of people and things than extraverts.

Jung also describes a second typological category – functions of consciousness. Functions are two pairs of opposite psychological preferences. The word preference refers here to something which is innate, like being left-handed or right-handed. While we can all use either hand we have a preference for one over the other. Jung identifies two pairs of functions: one pair identifying two opposing ways of gathering information; one pair identifying two opposing ways of coming to decisions.

One preference for gathering information is sensation (also known as sensing). Sensing types prefer to acquire detailed information through the five senses (sight, touch, hearing, smell and taste). Sensing types naturally turn first to observable facts and events. The other preference is intuition. Intuitive types prefer to acquire information by reference to overall purpose and meaning. Intuitive types turn first to trying to discern meanings, relationships and possibilities beyond the immediate data. According to Jung, while we all use both ways of gathering information within this pair each individual prefers one function over the other.

The second pair of functions is concerned with organizing these perceptions and coming to a judgement. These opposed functions are thinking and feeling. The thinking function decides impersonally on the basis of logical and objective factors. Thinking types prefer to come to conclusions and make their judgements objectively, logically and by applying general principles. The feeling function decides primarily on the basis of personal and social values. Feeling types prefer to come to conclusions and make their judgements subjectively, personally and by employing their own and others' values. Again, each person prefers one function over the other although we all use both functions.

At the heart of Jungian typology is the way the preferences for the inner or outer world, the preference for one of the perceiving functions and the preference for one of the deciding functions combine powerfully to produce a particular psychological type. Jung's basic theory claims that the eight types so formed – for example extraverted sensing types, introverted sensing types, extraverted thinking types or introverted thinking types – are useful ways of categorizing observed differences between people.

Jung's observations led him to the conclusion that for each individual one of their preferred pair of functions, either a perceiving or judging function, is dominant and is relied upon more than the other preferred function. A number of questionnaires have been devised to help people discover which of Jung's psychological types they recognize as describing themselves. The MBTI is the most widely used instrument in commerce, industry, the voluntary sector and the Church for enabling people to gain insight into their behaviour and ways of relating to others. This process was initiated by Katherine Briggs with the subsequent collaboration of her daughter Isobel in the middle decades of the twentieth century. Although not formally trained in psychology, they admired Jungian personality theory to such an extent that they developed themselves the tools they needed for statistical research and set about collecting a pool of items that would reliably point people to an understanding of their psychological type. A brief account of their story and of the history and development of the instrument is given in the foreword of *Gifts Differing* (Briggs-Myers, 1980).

The Myers–Briggs Type Indicator

The MBTI consists of a questionnaire which seeks to help individuals identify their psychological preferences for extraversion/introversion, sensing/intuition and thinking/feeling.

The MBTI has also introduced an additional pair of preferences. It shows how we prefer to relate to the outer world using either a judging or a perceiving function. This is the judgement/perception preference. A preference for using one of the judging functions (thinking or feeling) for dealing with the outer world indicates a decisive, ordered and systematic approach to relating to external reality. A preference for using one of the perceiving functions (sensing or intuition) for dealing with the outer world indicates a flexible, open and provisional approach to relating to outer reality.

The judgement–perception index, although implicit in Jung's writing, is an addition to Jung's basic concepts. Thus the MBTI goes a stage further than Jung and offers a revised theory of 16 psychological types. The MBTI also offers a theoretical approach to the hierarchy of use of the four functions for each of the 16 types, which has yet to be demonstrated empirically. A simple summary is offered here. A fuller description of the four MBTI scales is presented in the manual for the instrument (Briggs-Myers and McCaulley, 1985).

Further sophistication in Jung's model shows which of the preferred functions is dominant and which auxiliary, and which is used in the outer world and which in the inner world. This moves to a more complex level of type theory, the explanation of which is not essential to this introduction to the topic and the illustrations we offer for the relevance of psychological type theory for supervision.

We think the MBTI makes a useful contribution but we all know that human nature is much more complex, and the determination of our typology more subtle, than a simple theoretical and derivative arrangement of the functions would appear to offer.

The MBTI is the most widely used model derived from Jungian personality theory and the most researched. Several million copies of the indicator are sold worldwide each year. Discovering a type that fits offers new insights into self, relationships with others and self-development. Isobel Myers's aim in developing the instrument was to provide individuals with an economical and accessible summary of aspects of personality. A subsidiary aim was to help people understand and value difference, and to grow in appreciation of those preferences different from their own. Myers's philosophy led her to the main concern, which was to help people see others as different rather than strange, odd or even weird. Personal development within type theory assumes one is, and remains, one type throughout life. Yet as human beings we are able to (and should, Jung would say), develop our own true type and promote the integration of its opposite characteristics in our journey through life. The MBTI model only claims to be an aid to this process.

The strengths of the MBTI are that:

- People generally recognize their type;
- The emphasis is on the positive qualities;
- The descriptions are based on empirical evidence rather than theory.

A weakness is that most people can see themselves in more than one type description, and some people even in several.

Strictly speaking the MBTI is not a test in the common use of the term – 'indicator' is the usual descriptor. The approved process of follow-up is direct feedback to the person who has completed the questionnaire, offering them the reported type as a hypothesis for both consideration and confirmation or otherwise.

The MBTI is advocated in this book with slight reservations. There has been criticism of the instrument both in psychological circles and in the church community. Some criticism from within the church community is based on a discomfort with using psychological tools in Christian ministry. Some of these criticisms can be found in *Myers-Briggs: Some Critical Reflections*, edited by Kenneth Leech (1996, currently out of print). Perhaps some of the criticisms of the MBTI arise in response to a simplistic application of the instrument and also from overambitious claims for it by enthusiasts.

Professor Leslie Francis (2001) acknowledges that, in spite of the criticisms, the MBTI remains a rich source of theory available to practical theology to account for individual differences in religious preferences and experiences. Research using the MBTI to explore religious questions and personal prayer practices is able to generate new insight with practical implications for the churches. Our book does not seek to be polemical, but useful. It is this desire, with a practical and accessible focus, that motivates and guides us in considering the MBTI with training incumbents and curates. In the end the rich diversity of God's creation, including humankind, defies completely certain categorization, and reminds us that typologies are human constructs. They are not true or false, but more or less useful.

Leslie Francis has produced a shorter, user-friendly questionnaire which is designed to help people identify their preferences for each of the eight polarities in the model we have discussed above. The Francis Psychological Type Scales (FPTS, published in *Faith and Psychology*, 2005) are included as Appendix 2. If you would like to discover what the FPTS might tell you about your psychological type please turn to Appendix 2 and complete the questionnaire there. But before you do . . .

Would you like to estimate what your preferences might be for each of the pairs we have explained in this chapter: extraversion/introversion, sensing/intuition, thinking/feeling, judging/perceiving? One way to do this would be to ask yourself what expectations you may have for your curate, or potential curate. If you would find this an interesting exercise please read the next few paragraphs before turning to Appendix 2 and the FPTS.

Here is a list of preferences representing an expectation you might have about a curate. Identify the phrases below which are true for you and how many of them. Think of the lists in general terms rather than applying to a specific context or a situation in ministry.

List A I expect my curate to . . .

- easily form friendships with many different people
- find it easy to meet a lot of new people
- be an enthusiast
- have an active social life to recharge his/her batteries
- help to get things going socially.

List B I expect my curate to . . .

- work well in solitude
- be energized by inner resources
- find things out by him/herself (e.g. reading alone)
- be hard to get to know in depth
- be slow to reveal his/her feelings.

Did you agree with more items in list A or in list B?

List C I expect my curate to . . .

- be meticulous
- be practical in discussing ministry
- pay attention to detail
- prefer to understand by starting with facts
- respect church regulations in pastoral situations.

List D I expect my curate to . . .

- be imaginative and speculative
- be primarily concerned with transforming the world
- welcome visions for change
- start from the overall idea first then look at the parts
- think in abstract rather than concrete terms.

Did you agree with more items in list C or in list D?

List E I expect my curate to . . .

- be comfortable with sceptical analysis
- be more focused on justice than peace
- communicate truth more than enthusiasm
- not be influenced by his/her feelings about people
- think in a detached and logical way.

List F I expect my curate to . . .

- be more interested in people's feelings than their ideas
- be pastoral more than prophetic
- enjoy pleasing others
- have a clear awareness of her/his personal feelings
- value compassion above frankness.

Did you agree with more items in list E or in list F?

List G I expect my curate to . . .

- be organized and systematic
- have things decided and settled in advance
- be punctual about appointments
- work best when there are clear schedules
- find daily routine a comfortable way to do things.

List H I expect my curate to . . .

- be comfortable with a degree of chaos
- discover what he/she needs to do as he/she goes along
- pull things together well at the last minute
- respond quickly to the unexpected or unplanned event
- work flexibly and spontaneously.

Did you agree with more items in list H or in list G?

The following paragraphs offer you a chance to guess at your type preferences. The items in the lists have proved reliable and accurate in indicating the preferences of psychological type (Tilley, 2006).

Thus if you found the sets of expectations in list A more attractive in representing your own expectations than those in list B this would indicate you may be more of an extravert than an introvert, preferring to draw energy from the outer world rather than your inner world. If the reverse was the case you may be more of an introvert than an extravert.

If you found the sets of expectations in list C more attractive in representing your own expectations than those in list D this would indicate you may prefer sensing more than intuition as a way of receiving information. If the reverse was the case you may be more intuitive than sensing.

If you found the sets of expectations in list E more attractive in representing your own expectations than those in list F this would indicate you may prefer thinking more than feeling as a way of coming to decisions. If the reverse was the case you may be more of a feeling type than a thinking type.

If you found the sets of expectations in list G more attractive in representing your own expectations than those in list H this would indicate you may prefer an ordered lifestyle more than a flexible one. If the reverse was the case you may prefer an open and flexible lifestyle more than a systematic and ordered one.

In each of the paired lists of preferences, which set do you estimate is more like you than the others? If you wish to continue with discovering more about your psychological type preferences please turn to Appendix 2 and complete the questionnaire forming the Francis Psychological Type Scales before reading on.

Type preferences in supervision

Having summarized the MBTI™ and offered readers a chance to discover their own psychological type preferences we examine the role the different type preferences might play in the relationship of training incumbents and curates.

Extraversion and introversion

The work of ordained ministry is likely to be attractive to extraverts since it is immensely varied and the pastoral role is boundary-less in both time and scope. It might be thought surprising that such a vocation attracts more introverts (according to some research findings) than extraverts. Introverts may be drained by the social interactions demanded in ministry, and by a ministry that often requires people to move quickly and frequently between different tasks. Clergy are often heard to complain about the nature and regularity of interruptions from the telephone and doorbell during the working day. Extraverts are likely to respond more positively to interruptions. They may even seek them out as a way of energizing themselves during quiet and reflective periods or times of isolation. However, ordained ministry might be attractive to introverts because the role and day-to-day ministry allows them freedom to pursue their own religious quest and to follow their own internal values.

In the training context, extravert curates will find it harder to apply themselves to reflection alone, and are likely to value a conversation with their incumbent, while introvert curates are more likely to value time alone reflecting on their ministry. Extravert incumbents and curates might more easily see the value of engaging in the practical tasks of ministry than the value of a reflective supervision session. They need to guard their time for reflection against the insatiable demands of ministry in the outer world. Introverts on the other hand need to guard against the temptation to spend too much time in their inner world and to realize that at the end of the day something has to be done.

Sensing and intuition

Pastoral ministry might be considered more attractive to sensing types (S types), being focused on the here-and-now responsive concern for others. Sensing types are less attracted to the broader picture of meaning, possibilities, vision-making and future directions than intuitives. Intuitive types (N types) respond enthusiastically to the need for overall goals and change, and personal growth and developmental concerns. Oswald and Kroeger (1988) illustrate this from their studies with clergy in the USA.

In the training context a sensing-preferring training incumbent may be less sympathetic to an intuitive-preferring curate who wants to approach learning for ministry in a holistic and goal-directed way. A sensing curate might struggle to respond critically to an intuitive incumbent who wants to explore the meaning of ministry in theological reflection, preferring instead to 'just get on with the job'.

Clergy with a preference for sensing will need to guard against the temptation to nit-pick about details and to emphasize the unimportant details, and to remind themselves of the purpose and goals of their ministry. Those with a preference for intuition will need to guard against the temptations to neglect facts and details and to make simple things overcomplex.

Thinking and feeling

Thinking types (T types) are logical, dispassionate and analytical. They tend to be firm-minded. Such clergy prefer decision-making to be based on truth and to distance themselves from personal issues; they want to understand and explain religion and faith. Feeling types (F types) value relational warmth and personal encounter, and will draw out meaning by engagement and immersing themselves in the experience. Oswald and Kroeger (1988) hold that differences between the thinking and feeling dimension produce ongoing conflict between these approaches to faith: 'occasionally T-type clergy need help in getting their heart in order. Occasionally F-type clergy need help in getting their head straight.'

In the training relationship a thinking-preferring training incumbent may find a feeling-preferring curate's need for positive feedback and affirmation irritating and irrelevant to the performance of ministry. A feeling-preferring training incumbent might be surprised by, and fail to appreciate, the more objective and analytical approach to preaching of her thinking-preferring colleague and thus seek to change it unhelpfully. The next quotation illustrates the opposite situation of a feeling-preferring curate with a thinking-preferring incumbent. One curate wrote of her incumbent: 'He used knock-down arguments based on logic, and I was often left with the feeling that something was right but was unable to justify it in terms he would accept.'

Clergy with a preference for thinking will need to guard against the temptation to minimize the importance of people and their values and may want to remind themselves of the need to limit the search for objective truth. Those with a preference for feeling will need to guard against the temptations to overidentify with others and to avoid conflict at all costs. They may need to remind themselves that ministry is often about enabling people to get the task done and that giving honest feedback and being critical helps people as much as affirmation.

Judging and perceiving

There are two opposite ways in which people relate to the outer world. Judging types deal with the outer world in a planned, decisive and orderly way. Perceiving types prefer a spontaneous, adaptive and flexible way. Clergy with a preference for judging will be keen to schedule and organize ministry; they will tend to seek order by controlling and regulating their lives and parish life. Those with a preference for perceiving will be more curious and open to issues in ministry, even when decisiveness is appropriate. They will take longer to come to a decision than those with a preference for judging. In an organization such as the Church, with a long tradition of accepted ways of believing and behaving, perceiving clergy may be less valued by congregations, and yet they may produce a freshness and vigour in religious life as it seeks to live out the gospel in the current culture.

In the supervisory relationship a judging-preferring training incumbent might be likely to seek to plan and organize the curate's time, seeking to provide timetables, lists of work and both long- and short-term plans. This could be experienced as oppressive by a perceiving curate who wishes to take opportunities to learn and grow in ministry as these are presented in day-to-day work, even at the expense of fulfilling an orderly and coherent set of objectives in an agreed timescale. A judging-preferring curate could feel frustrated by what is seen as a delay by a perceiving-preferring incumbent in leaving decisions to the last minute and thus shortening the time for preparation.

Clergy with a preference for judging will need to guard against the temptation to be overconcerned for control and dealing with political issues and may need to remind themselves of the importance of being open to other ideas and listening to people. Those with a preference for perceiving will need to guard against the temptations of procrastination and indecision, and distraction. They may need to remind themselves that ministry is often about organizing things and people and about putting ideas into effect.

These psychological preferences are often put together in 16 combinations that indicate 16 different psychological types. The letters indicating each preference are used as a shorthand way of indicating a type, e.g. INFP and ESTJ (where N is used to represent the preference for intuition because the letter I is used for the preference for introversion).

With these illustrations it is concluded that personal preferences and styles indicated by psychological type will colour, and help to determine, the relationship between supervisors and supervised and the expectations each will have of the other.

Using the MBTI with training incumbents and curates may help each of them to predict areas of expected interest in ministry and styles of relating that need particular attention, and may also lead to an awareness of the possible levels of strain and stress attributable to the preferences of each type. It is our experience that differences of preference can lead to great problems unless understood and discussed.

What does research say about psychological type in supervision?

One of the writers of this book, David Tilley, conducted research with training incumbents and curates using the MBTI and reported his findings in 2006. He used two types of data: first, psychological type data collected from 175 pairs of training incumbents and curates in five Anglican dioceses; second, data from a questionnaire sent to over a hundred curates of that group.

The table in Appendix 3 shows that the psychological types most represented among curates are ENFJ (14.29 per cent), and ISFJ (12.57 per cent). The types most represented among the incumbents are ENFJ (12.57 per cent), ENFP (11.43 per cent) and ISFJ (10.86 per cent). The sample data are too small for completely accurate correlations of MTBI types of incumbents with curates. However, some of the findings listed below are interesting.

First, compared with each other there is broad similarity between curates and incumbents in respect of the type preferences for introversion and extraversion although curates marginally prefer introversion over extraversion.

Second, it was found that incumbents on the whole prefer intuition over sensing. Curates report similarly but slightly more than incumbents.

Third, incumbents prefer feeling over thinking, as do their curates but more than do incumbents.

Finally, incumbents prefer judging over perceiving as attitudes to the outer world. Their curates also prefer judging over perceiving as attitudes to the outer world, slightly more so than incumbents.

It is important to remember that there are no statistically significant differences between the two groups.

It is not claimed that the groups of curates and incumbents used in the research are representative of all curates and incumbents working together, still less of all clergy in the Church of England. Nevertheless if anything might be indicated by this finding it is that these data, limited though they are, might suggest a consistency of psychological type in the selection for ordination in the Church of England over a span of years, from the ordination of the most senior incumbent to that of the newest curate.

Psychological type preferences in working pairs

What might be predicted about a difference between type preferences in working pairs of supervisor and supervised? Let us look first at the possible consequences of being similar and different in type preferences.

Similarity of type will lead to good communication and a good working relationship. Insofar as there is a similarity of preferences, the curate and incumbent could be expected to recognize each other's strengths, to understand each other's approach to ministry and to communicate easily. Thus there would be less opportunity for misunderstanding and interpersonal conflict. However, similarity of type has some disadvantages in a working relationship. Such similarity might result in blind spots where aspects of a situation or issue are minimized or ignored. Similarity could also give rise to assumptions about the other person not being checked, and alternative points of view from other people, with different type preferences, not being given sufficient consideration. Members of a congregation with different type preferences from the clergy might feel unappreciated, or find it harder to offer their opinions. Similar type preferences might lead to competition between two ministers for ministerial work that suited the preferences they shared, to the exclusion of other priorities in ministry.

Difference of type will offer the opportunity for challenge and critique to each party, since different perceptions will stimulate other ways of understanding a situation or issue. A new curate with different type preferences could enliven and energize the ministry perspective of a parish and its incumbent which had become familiar, unchallenged and stale. People in the congregation with the same preference as the curate might feel that they are better understood, and that their opinions are better valued.

We can now predict how type preferences might colour the supervisory relationship. Brief reminders of the type preferences are included here. To those reading the whole of this chapter this might seem like repetition; nevertheless those who have skipped the basic sections introducing the MBTI model might find a few words describing the preferences in the context of supervision useful reminders.

The type differences for the perceiving functions as reported above for curates and incumbents are examined first. The data report curates in the sample preferring intuition over sensing and this to a slightly more significant extent compared with the incumbents.

The implications of difference in the opposite preferences for sensing and intuition in the supervisory relationship concern different approaches. The intuitive-preferring curate will want to start with the overall picture, to develop theories, to design solutions and to apply ingenuity to problem-solving. The sensing-preferring incumbent will want to start with immediately known facts, to focus on praxis and concrete situations, and to apply experience to problem-solving. (The opposite will be the case where the preferences are reversed.) The needs of the supervised should be taken into account by those who design learning programmes for ministry or supervisor, even though these preferences may be less comfortable for that designer. Without it, the motivation and commitment of the curate to learning from the experienced incumbent may be at risk.

Difference in the other opposite preferences for thinking and feeling in the supervisory relationship could lead to more misunderstanding and conflict. These preferences are concerned with the way decisions are made and what values are taken into account. In the research data reported here curates are more likely to prefer feeling over thinking, slightly more so than incumbents. Feeling types are likely to be more concerned for subjectivity; for harmony and creating and maintaining stable, trouble-free relationships. Thinking types will be more concerned for objective analysis and principles and for dispassionate values. Thus these different approaches to decision-making, and the outcome of the process, could lead to competition and conflict unless the two approaches are seen as valuable and contributing equally but differently to good decisions.

Good experience in this respect was reported by the curate who worked with an incumbent opposite on all four scales to her own preferences:

> He assumed I would work in the same way as him. As we got to know each other more his expectations of me reflected my personality. He didn't change how he did things – but he didn't expect me to do the same as him any more.

Judging and perceiving was one of the differences between this couple, who coped with it adequately. Nevertheless this difference offers a potential difficulty for curate and supervisor in the type preferences for attitude to the outer world. Experience has shown that a difference between these preferences can generate impatience and annoyance between curates and incumbents. Perceiving types will tend to delay decision-making until they are assured that all the information is to hand and will wait as long as possible. Judging types will tend to make decisions easily and early, even if such decisions are subsequently revised. For example, an incumbent with a preference for judging may require a more ordered, systematic and scheduled approach to learning about ministry than feels comfortable to a perceiving-preferring curate. Similarly, a judging-preferring curate may feel frustrated by an open-ended and more spontaneous approach to supervision taken by a perceiving-preferring supervisor. Because they are more open-ended it is easier for those who prefer perceiving to wind up those who prefer judging, who tend to be more decisive than vice-versa! Nevertheless judging types may well think that perceiving types are too laid-back or casual over things that matter. Thus the difference between perception and judgement provides insight into how people approach and respond to others in supervision.

It is encouraging to record another instance of positive attitude in respect of this difference offered by the curate, a perceiving type, who worked with an incumbent who was a judging type: 'There was considerable tolerance of differences and recognition of our different personality types.'

Other research findings from recent questionnaire to curates

In this discussion of psychological type in supervision some other research findings are worthy of note. Is there a relationship between type preferences and the national criteria for selection for ministry? There is some evidence for a relationship between type preferences and the personal qualities and attitudes appropriate for incumbents likely to be effective trainers of junior colleagues. The tentative conclusion from the curates' responses is that the extraversion–introversion scale is important in supervision. Incumbents with a psychological type preference for extraversion are more likely to conform to the criteria suggested by the Advisory Board for Ministry than incumbents with a preference for introversion.

Is there a relationship between type preferences and the way curates perceive their incumbents to have helped them to achieve the aims and outcomes for their training? The views of curates point to the conclusion that incumbents with a psychological type preference for extraversion and intuition are more likely to be effective in providing the appropriate training for curates. Thus there is a relationship between the type preference of supervisors and their effectiveness in enabling curates to develop the qualities of person and life and the associated skills that are required by the diocese for current and future ministry.

Turning to what curates said about their happiness and sense of satisfaction in their first post, there appears to be a positive relationship between the incumbents' preference for extraversion and what curates felt about their first post in ministry. It appears that incumbents who prefer extraversion are more likely to produce more satisfied and happy curates.

More research findings concerning the expectations incumbents have of their curates are discussed in Chapter 12.

It is not part of the purpose of this book to advocate, on the basis of these findings, the use of psychological type in the selection of incumbents to train curates. But the inference to be drawn from these findings is that self-knowledge and awareness of type could have a significant role to play in the preparation and training of those clergy selected to supervise curates. Having discussed how psychological type preferences affect the relationship in supervision the remainder of this chapter examines the other important model of difference, styles of learning.

Adult learning styles

The other model of difference helpful in supervision is the one which suggests there are four different styles of learning for adults and that each of us has one style of learning that suits us best.

- Do you know what your style is? Do you prefer to get involved in an activity in order to gain experience before considering it or evaluating it? If so, you are *an activist*.
- Do you find you learn more effectively if you watch or debrief an experience, or look back on something with which you have been involved? If so, you are *a reflector*. In this model reflector is used not to imply thinking reflection but rather the reflection from looking in a mirror.
- Do you like theories and do you like to know how and why before tackling a project? If so, you are *a theorist*.
- Do you find asking yourself 'So what?' and seeing practical applications of something helps you better to learn about it? If so, you are *a pragmatist*.

The theory suggests that we have a preference for one of these activities, and that personal growth and improved learning will come from increasing our familiarity and abilities with the other three styles. Let us now look at the origin and development of the theory and its implications for supervision.

David Kolb and Ronald Frey first drew attention to the different learning styles of adults in the United States (Kolb, 1984). The theory they originated was developed subsequently in the United Kingdom by psychologists Peter Honey and Alan Mumford (1986).

The learning cycle

David Kolb is famous for his introduction in the 1960s of his analysis of how people learn in the workplace and this has been the basis for a great deal of understanding about adult work-based learning. He noticed that while some people did in fact learn from their mistakes, others didn't, and he was interested in discovering

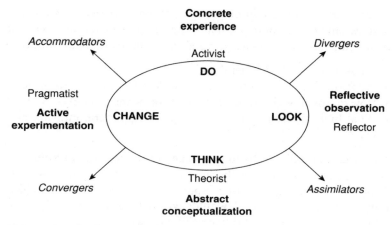

Figure 5.1 The learning cycle

what was different about the people who learned from their mistakes. Kolb developed a learning cycle that is now well accepted and used in many contexts. This learning cycle has four stages (Figure 5.1).

The first stage is called concrete experience. If we were using the cycle to learn about funeral ministry, concrete experience would refer to everything that you actually do with reference to taking a funeral: the visit; the planning; the funeral itself and whatever you do afterwards.

Kolb identifies observation and reflection as the next stage in a learning cycle. These processes are what you do afterwards in order to produce as rich a texture of narrative about the experience as you can before you do anything else. There are a number of sets of questions that can be used such as:

- Can you tell the story of your thinking and feeling as you visited the family, prepared the funeral, and conducted it and so on?
- What went according to plan and what didn't? Were there critical moments for you and for anybody else?
- What do you think people expected of you and how far did their expectations match your own?
- If there had been a fly-on-the-wall television camera through the whole experience what might it have caught on film that you didn't notice at all?

The third stage in a learning cycle concerns the development of theories, concepts and generalizations. This is the stage when, based on experience and careful observation of that experience, you begin to draw out generalizations and in this example, generalizations about taking funerals. For instance, the questions that might help would be:

- What makes a good funeral and why?
- What theology is used to decide what kind of sermon to preach?
- How do my thoughts fit in with the theories and teaching of others?
- What biblical teaching influences me in my funeral ministry and why?

This leads naturally to the fourth stage of the cycle, which Kolb calls active experimentation. In the light of my experience, my observations and debriefing from that experience, and based on generalizations I am making, how I would like to behave differently, plan differently, do the funeral differently? and so on.

Of course, learning can be haphazard and intuitive but there are a couple of points from this learning cycle to emphasize.

The first is that you can start in this cycle anywhere you like. For example, long before you took your first funeral you may well have thought about it quite a lot, read some books about taking funerals and developed some theories and generalizations about funerals. Or it may be that your first experience of funerals was as a member of a congregation so you spent a lot of time noticing what was going on. Or it may be you ended up having to do your first funeral because your incumbent was on holiday and you just had to get on and do it.

The second thing to stress is that while you may start in the cycle at any stage it is important that you follow the steps of the cycle in order. It is impossible to do any observation and the building of a rich narrative without the concrete experience first. Most theories and generalizations are flawed because they don't take account of all the information and observations that you have made. It is not much good changing your practice if you haven't thought about why you should do so.

So David Kolb's learning cycle is based on an action reflection process. Concrete experience and active experimentation move towards action, and reflective observation and abstract conceptualization move towards reflection.

All models of structured reflection adopt and build on this basic learning cycle developed by David Kolb. For a number of years in the Church of England network of trainers it has been renamed in the simpler: 'Do, look, think, change.'

Over the years people have worked at developing this simple cycle and linking it to a number of things. The first of these is in the area of realizing that people have different strengths and weaknesses as they engage in the different aspects of it. Some people have real ability in the theorizing part of the cycle, but seem quite uninterested in doing the observation, and can miss some very important aspects. This has led people – and in the UK, Peter Honey and Alan Mumford in particular – to identify learning preferences. This basic self-scoring questionnaire is used a great deal in initial and curate training to help people identify where their strengths as a learner are, and where they need to develop their skills. People who prefer concrete experience are called activists; those who prefer reflective observation, reflectors; those who enjoy theories, thinkers; and those who like to experiment, pragmatists.

One of the interesting aspects of this is that different educational methods focus into different aspects of the cycle, and we now know that your preference as a learner will attract you to different ways of learning. Theorists love lectures and reading but hate doing role plays, while activists will always be the first to jump into a novel learning experience. We have learnt also that our preference not only shapes the way we like to learn but also the ways we like to teach. Reflection in ministry is so important that we devote the following chapter to reflection and how to do it.

David Kolb also did work in this area and came up with different descriptors, linked these to career options and applied it to the recruiting of people into organizational roles.

People who sit happiest in between concrete experience and reflective observation he calls *divergers*, and says that they are very good at seeing things from all angles, are good at ideas and have a keen interest in people, being sensitive to the feeling world.

Assimilators are in the quadrant between reflection and theorizing and are good at creating theoretical models, inductive reasoning, assembling disparate observation into integrated explanation, and in shaping clear and precise theories.

Moving into the next quadrant, between theory and pragmatism, come *convergers*, who are very good at applying ideas, and can focus on specific problems with deductive reasoning. Convergers are better at using reason than emotional responses.

In the last quadrant between pragmatism and concrete experience are the *accommodators*. These people are good at doing things, carrying out plans, adapting to new circumstances, taking risks and doing intuitive problem-solving, and are better at relying on people for information than on their own analytic ability.

You will not be surprised to know that the Myers–Briggs Type Indicator has also been used to establish a the link between psychological types and learning preferences.

A useful summary is given in *Learning for Life* (Yvonne Craig, 1994) and reproduced below.

A description of the learning styles

1 *Experiencing*
   Whatever we do we filter new information through our memory banks of previous experiences. Reading this book is a handy example: what makes sense will be retained and threaded into our theories, changing our practice. Anything else will be rejected and forgotten since it strikes us as either irrelevant or inaccurate.

2 *Reflecting*
   But experience is not enough – as the Proverbs say, it may make a wise person wise but it also confirms fools in their foolishness. It may require deep personal stocktaking. The 20-year-old student weeps in his tutor's room because his divorcing parents have torn up his childhood history of a happy family life . . . now saying it was all a sham. A few years later he and they recognize that there was some truth in both stories: there was a great deal of happiness, but it was far from perfect. We ponder our experiences to make sense of a messy and complicated process, sometimes alone, sometimes one to one and sometimes in a safe group.

3 *Theorizing* (or reviewing)
   This is the time for drawing things together into a framework which makes sense, perhaps considering several options, choosing one and being able to justify the choice. This is where the theories and models come into their own as we hold each one up as a lens through which to view what is before us. At this stage we draw conclusions from the experience.

4 *Pragmatism* (or taking action)
   All of us (incumbents and curates) alike are changed in some way by the learning process. We may as a result make a conscious decision to do or be something different. It may be that we are testing out our conclusions to see if they work. If they don't we can drop them, if they do they become part of us. Either way our experience is new and the cycle continues.

Adapted from Craig (1994).
Slight changes have been made to the language to suit a context of supervision in ministry.

This is offered as a useful model, and it is helpful because it gives an overview and a reminder of stages of learning that might have been skipped. Nevertheless human nature and life is rather more haphazard and unpredictable than a superficial reading of the model would suggest. It would be good to attempt to discover your learning style by acquiring the Honey and Mumford learning styles and by completing the questionnaire. Having done that it is possible to ask, Is this me? Do I recognize myself here?

Learning styles in supervision – *in a nutshell*

How do we apply this model to the supervision of newly ordained ministers? Let us assume by way of illustration that guidance over the first funeral is needed. How might supervisors with preferences for the different learning styles approach the topic?

The activist supervisor will naturally *tend to help* by:

- generating opportunities for colleagues to take part straight away and reflect on what they do
- taking an optimistic and positive view of new suggestions
- responding spontaneously to opportunities for curates to gain experience
- take a chance on letting a colleague loose in a new experience.

Will naturally be *less likely to help* through:

- providing planned and sequenced parish experiences
- assessing and using learning experiences which are different from when she/he was a curate
- discussing experiences beforehand and evaluating them afterwards
- asking the curate to prepare a plan in advance.

Nutshell summary: An activist incumbent may assume a curate will learn in an activist way. 'There's a funeral later this week, have a go and then we'll talk about it.'

The reflector supervisor will naturally *tend to help* by:

- suggesting activities for observation ('Go and have a look at . . .')
- identifying ways in which experience can be debriefed
- discussing what might happen before an experience
- giving advice on preparation for aspects of parish ministry.

Will naturally be *less likely to help* through:

- offering ad hoc immediate learning opportunities
- putting curates in risky situations
- giving immediate answers to direct and unexpected requests for guidance
- providing a systematic overview of ministry in the parish.

Nutshell summary: 'I'm doing a funeral in a few days. Why don't you come and watch, and maybe video it so that we can spend a bit of time afterwards really looking at it in detail?' Afterwards: 'How do you think it went?'

The theorist supervisor will naturally *tend to help* by:

- offering an interest in theological and sociological approaches to the church and to parish ministry
- pointing out complexities which might be anticipated ('Have you taken into account . . . ?')
- pressing for clarity of structure and purpose
- moving on from specific instances to general principles in parish ministry.

Will naturally be *less likely to help* through:

- identifying personal factors and accompanying feelings in a situation
- using data or ideas which conflict with their theological attitude or ministerial stance
- showing how to use information he or she regards as important
- drawing up specific action plans.

Nutshell summary: 'Have a look at Wesley Carr's Brief Encounters *and we'll discuss it next week. I would also like you to read several other books and examine the funeral liturgies and write a short paper on how you understand the meaning of funerals in the life of the Church, especially with a reference to evangelism, and we will talk about it before you take your first funeral.'*

The pragmatist supervisor will naturally *tend to help* by:

- responding to the colleague's initiatives and suggestions
- being interested in specific plans
- being open to applications and the colleague's previous experience
- exhibiting belief in improving the way things are done.

Will naturally be *less likely to help* through:

- intellectual approaches to problems
- encouraging action for the long term
- using opportunities which he or she sees as divorced from real life or present church goals and culture
- encouraging interest in novel or unproven approaches.

Nutshell summary: 'Yes, you take this funeral, but come and check out with me first that you know what you are doing. Don't forget to brief the organist if you want the hymn in a different place, and make sure to press the red *button for the curtains. Watch the funeral director, he'll try and pay you at the door!'*

If you have discovered your own learning style you may think these applications are caricatures! However they serve to illustrate the different approaches in supervision that would result from each style. We all adjust our tendencies and preferences to suit the context, for example a minister who is naturally an activist may well perform in ways that suit other learning styles because that is appropriate. The learning styles are descriptive, not prescriptive. The important thing is to develop a holistic approach in supervision rather than constantly using one approach. You can try out a variety of approaches to find what suits your colleague.

This chapter has looked at how two models of differences between people contribute to good practice in supervision. There are other models, but these have been found to be particularly useful in a number of dioceses with training incumbents and curates. They offer a language which supervisor and supervised can use to explore and talk about difference. They affect approaches to the supervisory relationship and to the examination of ministry.

This chapter has explored two popular models of difference among people and the relevance each might have in supervision. The next chapter picks up the theme of helping others to learn introduced in Chapter 3, explores the role of reflection in learning and offers ideas for aiding and developing reflection between colleagues.

Points for reflection

- What sort of teacher do you think you are: a diverger, assimilator, converger or accommodator?

- How have the models in this chapter advanced your thinking about supervision?
- Could you explore these models with your colleague and discuss what changes you want to make in your expectations of each other?

6

Reflection: what it is and how to do it

- Do you naturally reflect about things?
- How have you helped someone to reflect – in pastoral care, in spiritual direction, in counselling?
- Are you aware of anything that prevents you learning from experience – a theological mindset, assumptions about your abilities to reflect, bad experience when reflection has made you feel uncomfortable?

In the previous chapter we looked at working with difference – differences of person, attitude and ministry which need to be recognized in your work of supervision with curates. In Chapter 3 we outlined the ideas and principles of adult education that are relevant and important in helping curates learn about ministry. Chapter 3 introduced the notion of reflection. How we make sense of our experience and let it inform decisions and future action will be the focus of this chapter.

Why is reflection important?

There is sympathy for busy priests who say to themselves, 'Oh dear, this may be useful, but it is hardly essential and it *must* be a low priority in the stressful life of a hard-worked, even over-worked, parish priest.' And we understand a view sometimes held by curates that the time for thinking and learning about ministry is past, 'We want to get on with being *useful* to people, to God's Church and our incumbent.' However, while we understand it, you won't expect us to agree entirely!

The implementation of the report *Formation for Ministry in a Learning Church* (Archbishops' Council, 2003) has already begun to see changes in the expectations of the national Church about continuing learning for ministry, of bolting together pre- and post-ordination education and training in a single whole. Although the changes will take a number of years to settle into a familiar pattern (and that at different speeds in different parts of the country) this new policy is already having an effect on understanding the role of the training incumbent.

We consider now the role of the incumbent in helping the curate reflect on the day-to-day ministry and so acquire learning for the achievement of goals. The place of reflection in ministry-based learning is thus examined. The work of ministry is based on human relationships and, in this sense, learning for ministry will require the practice of continuing to reflect on those relationships at the appropriate level. Reflection allows clergy to discover the meaning and the appropriate effective and practical responses to the dilemmas associated with the material, emotional, psychological and spiritual needs of parishioners.

There are a number of models of reflection on ministerial practice that commend themselves to dioceses and each diocese is likely to promote a particular way of doing it. One example, which we explored fully in Chapter 5, is the do-look-think-change sequence. We do something, or experience it. Then we look at all of it, examine it, and reflect back on what happened. Making sense of it comes next, thinking about how it fits into our scheme of things, making judgements about what helped or hindered. Last of all comes planning for future action. It may be that something could be better or just that the experience was worthwhile and worth repeating or recommending to others.

This simple sequence celebrates our capacity 'to respond rather than react' (Covey, 1982). Covey emphasizes the need to create space between something you do or experience and a response to it so that the experience can be 'digested' and an appropriate response made on the basis of consideration.

It might be in order to clarify what is meant by reflection in ministry before getting deeper into this chapter. Quite simply it means enabling a person to tell the story of something that was significant for them, to get hold of what happened before and during it and what the consequences were. This includes enabling people to discover what part they played, how they felt physically, emotionally and intellectually about it. Knowledge gives you control; and the greater knowledge about an incident or aspect of ministry that was significant makes it more likely that the good and effective might be repeated, and what was unhelpful and ineffective can be modified or avoided.

What is learned afterwards is based on the things noticed afterwards. I was more flustered than I thought. I don't know why I was so anxious. Why did I respond like I did? Becoming more aware of things later enables us to consider what we might have done and what effect that might have had. Both noticing and imagining what might be different maximize your ability to change.

It is a primary aim of supervision in the first years of ministry to inculcate and facilitate habits of reflection. Such an emphasis follows naturally from collaborative approaches to ministry and the changing nature of theological education. While there are many ideas and methods evolving in the field of theological reflection we are interested in encouraging and aiding that reflection which builds and maintains ministerial praxis. We firmly believe, with others, that the ministry of the Church today needs a proactive rather than a reactive style of ministry, no matter what has worked well in the past.

Teaching incumbents the skills for aiding reflection has been, and continues to be, a relatively recent development in the preparation and training of incumbents for the arrival of a junior colleague. The provision of training in the skills of supervision as part of the induction process for incumbents was introduced first in Lichfield diocese in the early 1990s. It has since been adopted by a number of dioceses. Training in supervision is provided prior to the arrival of the curate. This has sought on the one hand to offer a new self-understanding to training incumbents and on the other hand to develop skills of supervision that parallel those of others in the caring professions. It is the aim of supervision training to equip training incumbents with the skills of listening and questioning.

In this way it is shown that supervision has developed as a useful tool in the work of training the Church's priests – as part of the thoughtful and creative process of equipping unique individual people for ministry both in the Church and the world. Well-conducted supervision provides curates with tools for ongoing, self-managed learning and the skills of reflection associated with it ready for when they become incumbents or move to a second post in ministry. But it is important to recognize the boundary between supervision and therapy or counselling. While it is true that the primary tools for ministry are ourselves and our relationships, we must distinguish between the person and the role they inhabit. We looked more thoroughly at this in the previous chapter when we discussed personal differences between training incumbents and curates. Here it is sufficient to say that while the process of supervision may identify personal issues and responses, the supervision session is not the place to deal with them, nor is the incumbent the right person to assist with them. Issues that highlight the need for therapy of whatever sort need to be progressed elsewhere. The business of supervision most remain clearly focused on the practice of ministry – the work of the curate.

In the diocese of Coventry in 1999, incumbents spent 15 hours of contact time in training before the arrival of a curate. Six of these were occupied with the specifics of supervision. A further day's training was provided for incumbents and deacons three months after the ordination. This aimed either to kick-start supervision sessions between them or to fine-tune the process which had already begun.

Nevertheless, training incumbents have not always enthusiastically welcomed these new understandings of their role. Their own training incumbents did not always model these skills positively. Some have felt challenged to develop abilities that were not necessarily evident at the time of their selection as potential trainers. Thus while this shift of emphasis in the constituent role is desirable, in reality it has not always been complete, thorough or anything other than patchy. Gordon Oliver, Director of Training in Rochester diocese, reported a failure on the part of training incumbents to engage in regular supervision with their curates (Oliver, 2001). Elsewhere a curate reporting confidentially on his training at the point of moving on to a new post in the Midlands in 2000 said: 'Training in the parish was virtually non-existent – I used other incumbents in order to engage in reflection and evaluation.' On being asked specifically about the amount of formal supervision he received he wrote: 'Very little. Nothing was structured into the programme of the week because the incumbent was not good at keeping to a timetable.' On being asked how he had been helped to make the best use of his training parish he wrote in a confidential report made to one of the authors:

> I was asked what I would like to do in the parish. This meant I could get involved in certain projects or 'ministries' of my own choosing. I was not helped to think through areas of experience that would be valuable to me in the long term.

This experience is paralleled by that of curates in other dioceses reported both in Burgess (1998) and Harbidge (1996).

Reflection – what it is

Before offering processes and methods of how to reflect in ministry it is necessary to look at some ideas in order to understand just what it is.

The important work of Donald Schön was introduced in Chapter 3. Here we look at his thinking about reflection and also that of subsequent educators. Schön says there are two sorts of reflection – *reflection in action* and *reflection on action*.

Schön (1987) described his theory of reflective practice after studying a range of professions. He says (and some curates would agree) that formal education in preparation for working life is not always of help in solving routine, complex and indeterminate real-life problems. He maintains that unexpected events or surprises produce two types of reflection. When something does not fit our expectations, when surprises occur, then we respond by *reflection in action*. This is the process of making sense of the anomaly. Sometimes this reflection can be unconscious. Thus if learning from reflection in action cannot be described verbally then it can be neither taught nor, it might be claimed, evaluated. (Schön does not mention the role of imagination in reflection in action and it is possible that he ignores this important feature of reflection.) Imagination has the potential to offer a more thorough analysis of what has occurred, for example its causes and likely effects. Reflection in action occurs immediately. The phrase describes our ability to analyse and apply both past and present experience to unfamiliar events as they are happening.

Reflection on action is the name for thinking back on what happened in a previous situation, on whether what we did then was appropriate, and on how that situation may affect future decisions. In this sort of reflection we bring the advantages of distance and space to reflection. This less immediate and therefore more leisurely reflection potentially promises a greater reward. Here skills of synthesis and the creation of meaning come to the fore as people contemplate their experience and their future decision-making.

Schön claims that professional learning takes place as a result of both types of reflection. Each type has distinctive qualities; they are not just differentiated by being separate in time. Through the process of reflecting, both *during* their working ministry and *after* it, ministers continually revise and reshape their approaches, developing both new wisdom and sets of skills. Opportunities to engage with other learners, debriefing with peers, seeking feedback on a regular basis and journaling can all provide vehicles for a reflective ministry. We would add that reflection gives us the chance to ask, 'How does this fit with what I think God wants? How does it relate to pastoral care or further parish goals?' Without such space our ministry can become largely reactive – we allow ourselves to be determined by the last person who spoke to us, or we place ourselves at the beck and call of those who make the most noise. Thus it is that the authors (who acknowledge the need to practise what they preach) answer the busy priests we mentioned at the start of this discussion – reflection is important because it keeps us focused on the Kingdom of God and the priorities in ministry.

Levels of depth in reflection

One of the people who made a significant impact on the authors over the last few years is Jennifer Moon. In her book *Reflection in Learning and Professional Development* (Moon, 1999) she expanded and refined Schön's ideas and incidentally advanced the authors' own thinking considerably. Moon offers a model to describe the different degrees of depth in reflection and the effect and outcomes associated with each. The model constructs what she describes as a speculative 'map of learning' (Moon, 1999) (see Figure 6.1).

Moon claims that the stages of learning imply a progress through a greater degree of reflective depth each time, and that these stages are related to the way the learning is represented. The stages range from the simple noticing that something is different through several stages to personal transformation. The map is summarized as a way of characterizing progress in learning that has implications for the outcomes of learning.

The first stage is the simple noticing that something is different. Noticing is the stage of acquiring sensory data. Having acquired information, Moon claims that the learner moves to the second stage.

This is a process of making sense of the data; the data remain raw experience, which might be rejected as irrelevant unless some sense is made of that which is perceived. At this stage the new material is related to that which the learner already knows.

The third stage is one of 'making meaning'. At this stage the learner will have become sufficiently familiar with the material to explain elements of it because it has become integrated with the learner's cognitive structures. Up to and including this stage, Moon claims that the learner is in direct contact with the material. The first two stages are part of what Moon calls 'surface learning'. The third stage marks the transition from surface learning to what she calls 'deep learning'.

The fourth stage, which is well within deep learning, she calls 'working with meaning'. The learner now reflects on, or reasons with the

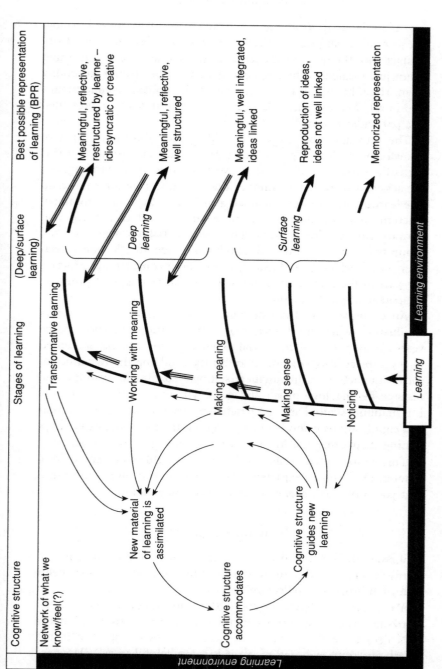

Figure 6.1 A map of reflective learning (after Moon)

new material apart from the physical source of the new learning. She gives the examples of reflection on a book or learning away from contact with the book or the teacher. At this stage the new learning is not just located in the cognitive structures, but begins to modify them. Here the significance of the material is considered and organized in relation to a particular purpose so that it can be represented in a particular manner.

The fifth and final stage, still within deep learning, is that of 'transformative learning'. As Moon defines it, transformative learning is the operation of persistent work towards understanding, but she acknowledges that at times a sudden transformation can occur. The learning may be accompanied at this stage by strong emotional reactions that are different from the intellectual excitement that may accompany earlier stages when a substantial new view emerges. Moon maintains that this fifth and higher stage of reflection is relatively rarely achieved, and usually not without considerable effort on the part of the learner. It is this stage, Moon claims, that produces the personal transformation.

An example from the experience of one of the authors serves to illustrate what Moon means by personal transformation. Some years ago he was studying social psychology and became interested in the subject of obedience to authority. Studying the dynamics of social interaction in hierarchical settings led him to examine and reshape his theology of sin and guilt. The images of the Amnesty International symbol and the paschal candle at Easter came together in a significant way and led to seeking out the local Amnesty group, joining it, piloting the formation of another group elsewhere and organizing sixth-form conferences on human rights for groups of local schools. Have you an experience of similar intensity and significance that you would call it one of personal transformation?

How do we do it?

The issue for the rest of this chapter is just how do you reflect in ministry and how do you help someone else to do it? What helps and what hinders in reflection?

We talked in Chapter 3 about the importance of asking open questions. Closed questions invite monosyllabic answers, usually either 'yes' or 'no'. Open questions encourage people to speak at greater length and with elaboration. So it is more helpful to ask, 'How are you getting on with the psychiatric patients?' – an open question – rather than, 'Everything's all right at the hospital, isn't it?' – a closed question. Asking and encouraging curates to offer illustrations or anecdotes to back up their remarks is particularly useful in preventing a conversation becoming excessively abstract and too general. Supervisors are not asked to offer condemnation or advice to curates. Occasionally a correction may be necessary, but this can be done without condemnation. Saying, 'This is what I would do if I were you', is less helpful and prevents the curate thinking it out for him or herself. 'What do you think you could do next?', 'What possibilities do you see for moving this on?' are much more creative. Of course, when curates are at a loss and need guidance and advice, the incumbent should feel free to offer it – but always last, and after probing that the supervisee really hasn't enough knowledge to know what the options are. Some curates will need a supervisor's support to grow in confidence that they are more competent than they believed.

Using questions to facilitate learning from experience

Guiding curates through a set of questions helps them to gain an overall appreciation of their learning, to express it and own it, and to gain confidence in their ability to devise a process for tackling something else. You will also signal that you are genuinely interested in the curate's development, and not just in another pair of hands to help in the parish. The overall message is to treat your curate as an adult who is highly motivated, very committed, self-directed and self-organizing. Some good questions, to structure reflection and avoid a haphazard approach which will depend on what is remembered in the moment, might be:

- What did you set out to achieve?
- What problems did you encounter?
- How did you overcome them?
- How satisfied are you with the results?
- What questions are you left with?

Other questions can of course be added, such as:

- What theological sense do you make of this?
- How does this connect with your initial learning for ministry?

A supervisor can best help by guiding a curate through a sequence of questions like these, and by asking follow-up questions to help the curate probe deeper into the experience. It is a quality of good supervisors that they know the questions to ask – and also when to keep silent. These skills cannot really be taught – they come out of the wisdom acquired by lived experience and from the maturity that has inculcated habits of reflection in supervisors.

The skill that *can* be learnt is familiarity with a range of questions to be deployed when occasion demands. Perhaps, as with spiritual growth, you can't take people further than you have gone yourself, and your own past and present experience of supervision will be useful here.

Some examples of good questions to aid reflection

In their book *Reflective Practice in Nursing* Palmer, Burgess and Bulmer (1994) suggest that the core question in learning from experience is: 'What information do I need access to in order to learn through this experience?' They give a further list of questions designed to elicit this information (see the example below). These are categorized under four subheadings: experience, reflection, influencing factors and learning. These questions are not a straitjacket to be used mechanically in supervision. They are given because they are good examples of an overview of the areas that might need to be reviewed and they remind the supervisor and supervisee of aspects that might be important on any given occasion. We see no reason why they should not be perfectly suited for use in helping curates to process and learn from an experience that is significant.

EXAMPLE 6.1 **Questions to help cover the ground in learning from experience**

Description of experience

1 Phenomenon	describe the 'here and now' experience.	
2 Causal	what essential factors contributed to this experience?	
3 Context	who else was involved in the background?	
4 Clarifying	what are the key processes (for reflection) in this experience?	

Reflection

1 What was I trying to achieve?
2 Why did I intervene as I did?
3 What were the consequences of my actions for:
   (a) myself?
   (b) the parishioner, person or family I was ministering to?
   (c) colleagues, team members, people I work with?
4 How did I feel about the experience when it was happening?
5 How did the people I was ministering to feel about it?
6 How do I know how they felt about it?

Influencing factors

1 What internal factors influenced my decision-making?
2 What external factors influenced my decision-making?
3 What sources of knowledge did/should have influenced my decision-making?

Could I have dealt better with the situation?

1 What other choices did I have?
2 What would be the consequences of these choices?

Learning

1 How do I *now* feel about this experience?
2 How have I made sense of this experience in the light of past experiences and future ministerial practice?
3 How has the experience changed my ways of knowing:
   (a) empirically?
   (b) theologically?
   (c) ethically?
   (d) personally (i.e. about myself)?

Adapted from Palmer, Burgess and Bulmer (1994). Slight changes have been made to the language to suit a context of ministry rather than nursing.

Another useful set of questions in helping curates who are taking up a professional role in public ministry is offered in Example 6.2.

EXAMPLE 6.2 Choose an experience or situation, and ask yourself . . .

- What was my role in this situation?
- Did I feel comfortable or uncomfortable? Why?
- What actions did I take?
- How did I and others act?
- Was it appropriate?

- How could I have improved the situation for myself, the person I was ministering to, my incumbent?
- What can I change in the future?
- Do I feel as if I have learned anything new about myself?

- Did I expect anything different to happen? What and why?
- Has it changed my way of thinking at all?
- What knowledge from theory and research can I apply to this situation?
- What broader issues, e.g. ethical, theological, political or social, arise from this situation?
- What do I think about these broader issues?

Adapted from Palmer, Burgess and Bulmer (1994). Slight changes have been made to the language to suit a context of ministry rather than nursing.

The last section of this chapter deals with some common barriers to learning from reflection on experience.

Barriers to learning from reflection on experience

Learning by reflection can be surprising, in that what you learn is unpredictable. Reflection leads to new ways of looking at something and by its very nature you cannot know in advance what it is you are going to learn. It doesn't work like other sorts of learning where you might decide – today I am going to tackle French irregular verbs. Nevertheless there are certain problems which people have observed to hinder or prevent the sort of learning we have been exploring in this chapter.

What is meant by barriers to learning? The phrase is used here to refer first to factors which are internal to the learner, which they bring with them to the process of reflection and which hinder the ability to reflect. For example, a previous unsatisfactory experience may mean that a person is unwilling to open themselves again to reflection on a similar incident because it is uncomfortable. Another example would be lack of skills or experience in reflection, or established ways of thinking which limit the ability of the imagination to look beyond and 'think outside the box'. There may be an inhibiting generalized message from others which we have internalized over time that tells us 'You can't do that', 'You are not clever enough.'

Second there are also barriers which are largely external to the person. Among them are pressure of time and other work demands, which result in a harassed and hurried approach to reflection, or a lack of preparation, or even a distance of time and space from the event being reflected upon. These make memory difficult or distorted. Facilitating the learning of others involves helping them to deal with any barriers they bring to the process of learning.

A recent thinker on leadership, Joseph Badaracco, says that for leaders, sound reflection is not a matter of time out; it actually involves the quality of their 'time in'. The best leaders do not approach their work as rational decision-making units whose humanity is the source of biases, weaknesses and distractions. Instead, they work as full human beings, whose feelings, instincts and often messy assessments of problems are genuine sources of wisdom and strength.

Badaracco (2006) says good deliberation is a messy process. It goes back and forth, zigzagging among feelings, thoughts, facts and analysis. It is discursive, rather than linear. It does not forget the past. It also looks forward, with vivid imagination, to possible consequences. He also emphasizes that emotions play a complicated role in good reflection. If they are too strong they make reflection impossible, but an emotional void is just as dangerous.

Badaracco quotes Sophocles who strongly suggests that good reflection, for individuals and especially for leaders, is the equivalent of sitting at the centre of a spider's web and vigilantly sensing what is happening along many different dimensions of a situation.

The extract below gives a list of barriers to learning from experience that we have adapted and drawn from the chapter written by David Boud and David Walker in *Using Experience for Learning* (Boud, Cohen and Walker, 1993).

Boud, Cohen and Walker go on to offer four steps to easing or transforming these barriers. The first is to recognize that they may exist. This is the start of dealing with them.

Some common barriers to learning from experience

- Presuppositions about what I can and cannot do
- Not being aware of my assumptions about my abilities
- Past negative experiences
- Expectations of others: peers, figures of authority, family
- Threats to my view of myself, my world view, my theological frame of reference
- Lack of self-awareness
- Inadequate preparation
- Hostile environments, or competing pressures
- Lack of opportunity to step aside from the task
- Lack of time
- Lack of support and encouragement
- Lack of skills for noticing and being objective
- Purpose which is unclear or unfocused (why am I doing this?)
- Established pattern and habits of thought and behaviour
- Inability to see value in the process (this is not real learning)
- Stereotypes about how we learn
- Fear of failure, fear of others' opinions, lack of self-esteem

Adapted from Boud, Cohen and Walker (1993), p. 79. Slight changes have been made to the language to suit a context of ministry.

Second they need to be named; that is, described and articulated to others. The more easily we can do this the more easily they can be made less powerful. Voicing our fears and inhibitions about learning diminishes their power over us.

Third, exploring the origins of our barriers – recognizing which come from within ourselves, which we have been 'given' by others, which are part of the social, educational or family background to which we belong(ed). Being clear about where the barriers come from helps us to discover what we can do to minimize them or overcome them.

The fourth and last step involves working with the barriers. Bringing the barriers, our assumptions and presuppositions, into the present light places them in a new and different situation and can lead to transformation.

Sometimes the barriers need to be confronted – if we have always believed that we couldn't do something, the best way to deal with it is to act as though we can do it, and to own the feelings that arise from taking a stance like this.

Barriers to learning such as those listed above can be very powerful, limit our lives and narrow our perspective of what is possible with God. But entering into new and unfamiliar territory may be best achieved when we are accompanied on the journey. Awareness of some of the barriers to learning will enable training incumbents to encourage, support and facilitate the growth of the curate when that is appropriate, not only as a priest or deacon in public ministry, but as a person and child of God. A 'cairn' in Jim Cotter's *Night Prayer* may be familiar to some: '. . . look at everything and think about it and communicate with the heaven that dwells deep within you and listen inwardly for a word to come.'

Turning this into a voiced prayer to the Spirit who will be our guide and lead us to peace and to glory could be a useful way for an incumbent and curate to begin supervision as they open themselves to the unique reality of the other.

Evidence of the seriousness with which training of curates is to be taken in the Church of today comes from Bishop Michael Turnbull in the foreword to *An Introduction to Christian Ministry* where he writes of ministerial priesthood as: 'a singular vocation, which requires its own special preparation and training and which is confident of its role amidst all the tasks which the Church is called upon to fulfil' (Kuhrt, 2000: ix).

Thus it is argued that the pastoral care of parishioners requires no less than the continuing reflection by clergy in the deepest of those levels described by Moon. We are persuaded that this reflection should be aided and supported by effective supervision. Very simply, this chapter has emphasized that the purpose of supervision is to help people notice what they haven't already noticed, because we all have limitations to our expectations and are bounded by our assumptions. The next chapter will look at how to get started after a colleague is ordained.

Points for reflection

- Reflect on what might be good questions for you to encourage and help a curate to learn from experience.
- Ask again what skills and abilities you might need.
- Do you need to sharpen your confidence to ask the right questions – if so how will you do this, and maybe with whom?

- If you already supervise someone can you discuss what specifically helps them reflect to learn from experience? Can you ask them how you might help better?
- What barriers to learning from experience are you now aware of in yourself? Can you voice them, discover their origins and rob them of their power over you?

7

There are varieties of curate!

- What sort of supervision can you offer to a curate specializing in sector ministry?
- Do you feel competent to supervise both the development of general skills of ordained ministry and the area of specialism?

This book is written with the traditional model in mind, which is still normative in most dioceses. However, God calls men and women to varieties of work in ordained ministry, and gifts them for the particular arena or focus of a sector or specialist ministry, as well as calling people to leadership in congregations within the traditional parish system. There are curates who work part-time in the parish, curates whose primary focus is at work, ministers in secular employment (MSEs), youth ministers and more recently we have seen the development of ordained pioneer ministers in many dioceses of the Church of England.

The tradition of the Church of England is of offering a generalized ministry based on communities of home residence. Both Church and nation expect clergy to be able to conduct occasional offices for rites of passage and to acquire the ability and skill to shape and lead public worship and to exercise leadership within the Christian community. Most dioceses seek parishes for the newly ordained that can provide for a range of experience (although there are rare exceptions). But of course even within this traditional pattern there are varieties. Each parish has its own particular context, and each community has its own set of expectations of the local church, and thus the shape of the ministry offered may be radically different.

Although this traditional model still 'works' in many places it has always produced dilemmas for those whose calling and skills are more specifically focused. Social changes in recent decades have challenged a purely traditional model of ministry to settled residential communities. There are other networks and levels of community which can be more important in shaping people's sense of identity and belonging. To take a simple example, an MSE quotes a common experience of people bringing in holiday snaps and family photographs to the workplace, and of people wanting to celebrate personal and domestic events with work colleagues rather than purely with relatives. For some people the work network may be more personally significant than their family. There are communities of leisure, and of different age groups and networks, where even physical contact is rare (e.g. Internet networks), though whether 'community' is the right word remains to be seen. This is not the place to discuss social changes or even missionary strategy other than to note that increasingly people are being ordained to minister in such contexts and to such groups, and therefore supervision for such ministers brings with it distinctive issues and needs. Increasingly for a number of new ministers, youth ministers, pioneer ministers and MSEs the traditional model is less than adequate. We look in turn at this variety of vocation among curates and examine supervision in this context.

Part-time parish focus

There are a number of people who feel called to offer themselves in the parish in a part-time capacity. Some of those are people who do not need to go out to work, as another member of the family is the main source of income. There are others who have retired early from secular employment, and others who are in full-time employment. They, as curates, will see their role mainly as assisting their incumbent, or ministering alongside him or her in a collaborative ministry team.

The main issue concerning supervision is the issue of availability. The problem is of the newly ordained acquiring enough experience of one particular ministry, say, conducting funerals, for the appropriate knowledge, skills and processes to be become familiar and internalized. Without a sufficient range and frequency of ministry each new occasion becomes a demanding one-off, with little experience in the background to provide a framework or guide. This was illustrated by the problems of the stipendiary rural curate described on p. 92. While each funeral is in a sense unique and needs to be personalized there are common factors, processes and systems that can resource and structure an approach to each.

This problem of availability needs to be sympathetically approached by training incumbents. We look at the supervision of MSE curates below, but one of our correspondents provided a telling illustration:

[My conscientious incumbent] repeatedly lamented that large chunks of my training were incomplete or non-existent because I was not available to undertake parish visiting (something he felt was extremely important), or to take part in the round of pre- and post-funeral visits and baptismal follow-up.

Even in a parish-focused ministry, similar frustrations can be felt where allowance has not been made for the limited time offered, and also where expectations do not suit the situation. As this report illustrates it can be as much a matter of priorities as it is of availability.

Pioneering ministers

We now have designated training pathways for those whose calling is to be ordained priests working mainly with young people, and for pioneer ministers. These new 'foci' (that's a Ministry Division term) of ministry have arisen alongside the publication of *Moving on in a Mission-Shaped Church* (Church of England, 2005) and have been keenly encouraged by the Fresh Expressions initiative <www.freshexpressions.org.uk>. Youth ministers and others pioneering new ecclesial communities might feel constrained by traditional models of Christian community. Supervision for these men and women needs to be sympathetic to risk-taking and new assumptions about ordained ministry, experimental though they may be.

Dilemmas arise from the desire to establish patterns of public ministry which while not bound to traditional social structures are also free to create and respond to new patterns of community and thus of mission.

Supervision into pioneering places needs to be supported by placements in situations where more traditional expectations can be met. This may seem to reverse the often usual pattern of stipendiary curacies. It is still important for pioneer ministers to have experience of meeting older shapes of social expectations. It is a question of 'both and' and is challenging both for supervisor and supervised.

As well as being provided with a sympathetic training incumbent, pioneer ministers will need supervision that is required to meet distinctive needs. For example a pioneer may be financially supported by the diocese at the time of being ordained and may be expected to research and develop funding for 'stipend' as well as their field of work after a few years. Discrete skills like this don't come with ordination and may require specific training and/or mentoring. Nevertheless a wise incumbent will want to support and celebrate one who is called to earn their own living while being ordained.

One significant difference attaching to the new ministries is the long-term expectations of the shape of an individual's ministry. Hitherto the normal pattern for full-time curates has been to move after three or four years into a post of first incumbency or similar. From there they may feel free to change direction and move into chaplaincy in hospital, armed forces or school for example. These new ministries call into question the assumption that a time of incumbency or sole charge is necessary or even helpful. Pioneer ministers may feel that they are called consistently to pioneering ministry and be ready to move from one pioneering situation to another without ever feeling the call to a more traditional parish ministry. Others may assume that after a time of pioneering they wish to enter a more traditional model of ministry. What matters, whether they stay or move into a more traditional form, is that people are able to lead and model the redeemed community in some sense with a consistency that is recognized both within and outside the Church.

Ministers in secular employment

Some of the newly ordained are called to exercise their ministry as priests primarily in their place of work – often a secular institution and environment. They may not be concerned to create ecclesial communities but to offer in the first place a prophetic and representative ministry in a secular context. The concept of MSEs grew out of the sort of thinking that gave rise to industrial mission. There are now many models of industrial mission and on the whole MSEs see their witness in their place of work to cover areas such as bringing the concept of the Kingdom of God to bear on ethical practices and policies within the organization's structures, as well as offering pastoral care to their colleagues. For others the personal conversion of the workers and the support of church-attending Christians in the workplace will be important, but for many MSEs these things are secondary.

MSEs have been around in the church for several decades and so are not as new within the structures of training and ministry as are pioneer ministers, and what we have learned about supervision in their first years of ordained ministry may be helpful for other pioneering ministries although, of course, there will be differences. MSEs are often misunderstood and do not feel properly accepted among those who hold more traditional models. While the canons of the Church of England remain unchanged it is possible to be ordained only with a licence to an ecclesiastical office, and at the moment these are restricted to a parish, university, school, theological college or religious community. Often, these days at ordination services the secular employment of MSEs is mentioned but there also has to be an ecclesiastical office and nearly always it is the incumbent of the ecclesiastical office who is the training incumbent.

All Christian men and women are involved in bringing their faith to bear in the secular spheres in which they conduct their decision-making. We all have to make ethical choices about the way we spend our money, the way we vote and to be informed about ethical issues facing society in general. The crucial question for many MSEs is what it means to be a priest at work. It is not about creating ecclesial communities in the workplace. Nevertheless supervision needs to be balanced. Where priests are known to be such at work they often become involved in offering pastoral care to colleagues and find themselves asked to assist in occasional offices for colleagues or their relatives. The newly ordained MSE needs to learn what one correspondent's incumbent called 'priestcraft'; although there are unlikely to be many calls to conduct a funeral or hear a confession it is essential to be able to respond to the request with confidence when it comes. Thus they need to be recognizably priests of the church; supervision from a parochially focused training incumbent can offer much, but can only go so far.

The MSEs who corresponded with us all affirmed the idea of supervision for their primary focus at work. It is such a special area – bringing the Kingdom to bear in secular organizations – that many training incumbents, even if they are sympathetic to the principles, do not have the background, skills, language or range of theological concepts to offer adequate support and supervision. Most MSEs will need to find supervision for what is often a lonely ministry on the margins from among other MSEs. Some dioceses sponsor and support groups of MSEs meeting regularly for support and theological reflection; this is a direct consequence of being licensed by the bishop. There is also a national network with which the newly ordained should be encouraged to be in touch. The quality of theological reflection in such forums as these is frequently of a high order.

In the first few years after ordination MSEs will also benefit greatly from one-to-one supervision with an experienced MSE; indeed we would argue that it is essential. It may seem that, as well as the ministry demands of the parish to which they are licensed, this is another time-consuming burden. Nevertheless if they are to be effectively supported by the Church and the effectiveness of ministry at work is to be maximized, supervision of this sort is necessary. This was an overall affirmation of those who corresponded with us.

One MSE wrote that the bishop had provided a mentor in addition to her training incumbent. She added that unfortunately the mentor chosen was very busy and was able to offer only general support rather than informed reflection on things as they came up. Clearly it is important for mentors not only to be theologically literate and to have knowledge of MSE ministry, but also to have the time to mentor effectively. A monthly meeting for this purpose would seem to be advocated in the first three years.

In order to avoid confusion of roles and responsibilities it may be useful for the two types of supervision to be distinguished by different names. Supervisor would be a good name for the role of the training incumbent since it implies an overall responsibility and a level of accountability. Mentor could be an appropriate name for the one who supports reflection on the non-parochial specialist setting. A mentor is generally understood as someone who has walked the course previously and who walks alongside a more junior colleague offering support and guidance, but has no formal reporting responsibility. A mentor for an MSE doesn't need to be ordained, but he or she does need to have facility with MSE theological concepts and praxis. However it clearly helps if the mentor happens to be ordained, because that gives added opportunity for understanding the nuances of how the role in the workplace is being inhabited. The sine qua non of the mentoring relationship is the ability to offer the newly ordained both informed support and challenge. As one correspondent wrote: '[A mentor] should be able to understand the essentially prophetic nature of ministry in secular employment and be able to help the trainee become accustomed to the isolation and discomfort that this involves.' Workplaces are very different and cultures in organizations vary; thus not all experience is transferable, so direction is inappropriate for this role – another reason why mentor is the better word.

Of the qualities required in incumbents of curates occupying a distinctive non-traditional role, clearly understanding and empathy are essential. An incumbent who is able to visit the workplace and see and experience the work of an MSE curate will be better informed than one who hears about it second-hand. One correspondent suggested that the job description for the secular employment should be attached to the working agreement. In this way sight of the primary focus is not lost under the pressure of familiar thinking. The incumbent must at times be able to interpret to others the nature of the role and defend the curate from ill-informed criticism. This will be especially important where a pioneer or an MSE curate enters a parish with a history of more traditional curates. A clear recognition of the limited time for traditional ministry is also important. Such an incumbent will want to help the curate develop a pattern of prayer life that suits them rather than imposes traditional expectations. The newly ordained will need to find a spiritual director who is able to understand the role; and a training incumbent may offer useful guidance from their more diverse knowledge. The training incumbent should be open to the limited remit of her or his training responsibility and not see the mentor as a threat or as a competitor.

Points for reflection

- This chapter may not have addressed all the relationship issues that arise for incumbents and curates with specialist ministries. What are your specific concerns?
- How do you seek support in addressing them?
- Do you need to explore even more the nature of your curate's specialist ministry in order to offer adequate defence and support when necessary?

8

Getting started

- You have prepared for the arrival of the new minister. Is there anything left to be thought about – have you considered whether he or she needs any guidance on what to do in the first week after the ordination? Have you talked this through together?
- How much time do you think a curate should spend on work?
- Have you talked about putting your expectations of each other into a contract, especially as regards supervision?
- Does your diocese have a handbook for training incumbents and curates? If so, is it worth looking at it again to see if there is anything you've forgotten?
- Are you being mentored as a training incumbent yourself? If this is your first curate do you need to check anything out with someone with more experience?
- As your potential curate goes on the ordination retreat have you considered any support their partner may need in perhaps a new home, new place, and especially if there are young children?

Chapter 6 was concerned with the theory and practice of reflection in ministry. This chapter will focus on starting your working relationship and preparing for the future. It will contain three sections: the transition from student to ordained person, contracting the working agreement and the supervision session.

Because this chapter is concerned with starting public ministry and we are writing from the context we know best some of it will be specific to an Anglican context. We hope nevertheless readers from within other traditions will find it useful.

Memories of what it was like when you started public ministry, all those years ago, could be flooding back. But it is worth reminding yourself that this is a different parish, a different climate for ministry, a different person being ordained, and you are different from the person you were then. You will also be drawing on the experience and wisdom you have acquired in the intervening years.

Nevertheless your curate will have a sense of excitement, a sense of ending a journey to ordination and starting a new journey, of anxiety about being up to the challenges, of fear about making mistakes, and a sense of a fulfilling moment in a vocation.

The transition from student to professional, from ordinand to ordained minister

Most centres of initial training for ministry seek to involve the supervising minister in at least one visit so as to facilitate transfer and impart useful information. It is very much to be hoped that potential training incumbents will be able to take advantage of the invitation. It will provide useful background on the prospective curate's studies and growth and it will feel very affirming for him or her. A final report on Anglican ordinands is also made available to the incumbent, usually from the diocese. There may be different procedures about transition in other churches.

The transition from student to professional is always a time of mixed emotions, of bereavements and new relationships. One of the significant losses is that of the college or course community. Suddenly the curate is alone, in a new role, in a way that she or he has never been before. That group of people who have studied together, with whom they have shared ideas, questions, doubts and problems, with whom they have moaned and rejoiced is no longer there. Of course there is the telephone and e-mail, but the curate may never see some people again. Now it is different; the loss is significant and the newly ordained year group may not have settled into new patterns of friendship yet. There will be fewer signposts and where to look for them may not be clear. The curate is likely to be dependent on you in a way which may be unfamiliar to you if you have not had a curate before.

There is a delicate matter of debt and financial stress. Stipendiary curates who have completed residential training, especially where married and with children, will have willingly made significant financial sacrifices. The stipend may not arrive for some weeks after moving in. It is not unknown for cases of hardship in families to create real strain. Many dioceses will be willing to make arrangements for an advance on the stipend, and cases where additional help is needed should be referred to the relevant archdeacon. Incumbents may want to ask caring and sensitive questions and to broker help from other sources where this might be appropriate.

It is unlikely that you will expect your colleague to preach in the evening of the day of ordination. It is worth saying that it is highly undesirable for them to do so, because it *has* actually happened; a deacon was asked to 'preach himself in and introduce himself to the congregation'. The newly ordained will need space and time to digest the emotional impact of the day, perhaps to say farewell to relatives from afar, and to reconnect with the family if married.

What about the next day? Some curates will want to get on with the job immediately. Others, especially some stipendiary ministers, will be grateful for a bit of time to continue the process of settling into a new house, sorting the study and helping to settle the children in a new school. You can't go wrong if you discuss how to occupy the day after ordination with your curate! You are unlikely to go wrong by giving him or her at least the morning off.

One diocese gave groups of incumbents an exercise in planning the first fortnight after ordination as part of their own preparation. It was found to be a useful exercise in which incumbents sorted out some ideas about phasing in ministerial experiences, making judgements about time off and thinking about the significant people and groups to which the curates should introduce themselves.

The transition from being a student to being a professional minister increases for the individual the range and depth of Christian ministry. This experience will be the seedbed for new learning. As book learning moves aside to make way for making sense of experience, working under your guidance and opportunities for reflecting with you will become more significant. The curate will look to you to help her or him with the important stages of articulating and internalizing learning. Doing theology together will be one of the stimulating rewards you receive from having a curate as colleague. Theological reflection is not always easy and we come to it with different hopes and fears. This is discussed more fully in Chapter 10. Unless you have supervised a curate before you will both be learning how to do this together. But it will not happen unless you create a framework together – a contract of expectations that you have of each other, a timetable for meeting and a programmed introduction to new ministerial work.

We turn now to the issue of creating that framework, the contract or working agreement. All dioceses will have a handbook or set of expectations for curates and incumbents. It may contain a sample job description and working agreement, a model of supervision and guidelines and requirements about reporting procedures. This chapter will explore how all these things are negotiated by training incumbent and curate.

Contracting the working agreement together

Clarifying your expectations of each other and negotiating a contract is not just about practicalities but about building a relationship based on mutual trust and respect.

Praying together

It would be extremely odd if an incumbent and curate did not want to pray together, both in intercession for their shared ministry and the people with whose care they were charged, but also to adore the God who has called them into discipleship and into a working relationship.

Depending on personal inclination and traditional patterns, for some this will be a regular sharing of the daily office, for others perhaps a Bible study and shared prayer time. It is important that working colleagues support each other in their devotional life separately from public worship. In public worship others are dependent on them for seeking to engage with God; together they need to express their own dependency on God and seek to be refreshed and nurtured by God. In a busy parish life, the discipline of meeting together regularly for prayer is something that both supervisor and supervisee should find helpful. It would be good practice that this should be in church as much as possible, perhaps in a multi-centred benefice moving round each place of worship in turn. Even if one is prevented from attending, the prayer should still be offered in the time and place agreed by the other(s). In rural benefices, time for travel will be an additional demand on ministry, but without a regular life for prayer for the incumbent and curate the newly ordained person could feel very spiritually isolated, unsupported and lonely.

Leading public worship

Discussion about opportunities to lead varieties of worship, where and when and how often, should be included in preparing the agreement. This will depend on the traditions of the parish, the curate's experience, the environment (rural, urban, etc.) and other factors. Most curates will want to experience the whole range as early as possible. It is customary in most dioceses that deacons should not preach more than two new sermons each month. The pastoral occasional offices are also included in this category. In parishes of sizeable populations, opportunities for baptism and funerals will occur regularly and frequently. It may not be the same in some rural and town centre parishes.

A case study will illustrate some problems in rural benefices of small populations. One curate, during the deacon's year, was assigned non-eucharistic worship on Sundays in the benefice. The unintended result was that although he met with the incumbent regularly for prayer he rarely received the sacrament on Sundays, with parishioners, and usually had to attend a weekday Eucharist, which wasn't always easy in the situation. Everyone thought that this was undesirable.

The other effect of the way service leading was arranged was that he hardly ever had an opportunity to observe the incumbent, nor the incumbent to observe him on Sundays. This was also undesirable and he felt more unsure of his developing skills than others in his year group because he didn't have the benefit of a critique.

Meetings for supervision

Where, when, with whom, frequency and type of meetings need to be agreed. First it should be specified which meetings are staff meetings, and which are supervisions private to the curate. Table 8.1 offers research findings on the experience of curates. Given all we have said about the importance of time devoted to learning and the importance of reflection in ministry, it is of concern that only 60 per cent of curates in the sample felt that their incumbents thought separate time should be devoted to supervision.

Concerning frequency and regularity: to be effective, supervision needs to take place on average about every three or four weeks. It will be more useful to the curate if sessions are more frequent in the first year than in the last year. It might be that every two weeks after ordination is desirable, graduating to every four or five weeks

Table 8.1 The integrity of supervision – incumbents' practice

	Agree	?	Disagree
My training incumbent demonstrated a willingness to distinguish staff meetings from personal coaching / supervision sessions	60%	17%	24%

in the final year. It suits some pairs to go away periodically for a day together. The risk is that the boundary between managing parish business and supervising learning gets eroded in favour of the former, and the immediacy of events is lost to the process of reflection. Most people are likely to find that less and more often is more useful than infrequent sessions of considerable intensity.

Timing

Each session needs to be an hour and a half. Sessions should be arranged for a time of day when there is minimum risk of interruption and when other commitments are least likely to crop up. It is probably helpful if a day and period is chosen when both parties are not tired, or hungry, or anxious about getting to the next appointment.

Venue

Where to hold the sessions – curate's home, incumbent's vicarage, neutral ground (e.g. parish office or meeting room)? The answer will depend on each couple. As a general rule the curate's home is much less desirable, so that afterwards he or she can walk away leaving difficult sessions behind if necessary. The likelihood of interruptions may be a factor – protection from young children, callers at the door and the telephone are important considerations. Both parties should avoid the temptation to invite others to contact them during the session because they know where they will be. An incumbent and curate assured a CME adviser that it suited them to conduct their supervision sessions over lunch in a pub. He was not convinced, and suspected there was collusion to avoid both the work of supervision and serious issues, and also to minimize demands on the incumbent's time. A secure venue is very important if the curate is to feel free to share feelings, problems, questions and confidential material. If another curate lives nearby perhaps a reciprocal arrangement might be made whereby each pair provides accommodation for the others to meet.

People involved

On the whole this will be a session for the newly ordained and his or her supervisor in private. However there may be occasions when it is effective to have others present – a team vicar, a youth worker, a reader or lay minister. This situation should be agreed and the purpose of the meeting should be clarified in advance between incumbent and curate.

Preparation and note-taking

Appendix 7 offers a proforma which a curate could use to prepare for supervision and facilitate the effective use of time. One incumbent may expect a reflection sheet to be sent ahead of the session each time; another may suggest it for anticipating a complex issue. It will depend on what suits the participants. Generally it is helpful to busy incumbents to know what the main focus of each session is likely to be. Similarly who keeps any notes and whether records are shared should also be discussed and agreed.

Becoming ordained in Anglican terms is to enter a complex set of relationships with levels of responsibility in different directions – to incumbent, the parishioners, the curate her/himself and to the bishop and diocese. There may be tensions and competition for priority and loyalties one way or another. In such a loose structure as the Church, compared with other professions, setting up the relationship properly is time well spent and is easier than sorting it out or building it as you go along. That way lies confusion and uncertainty.

Meetings and ministry beyond the parish and in the community

Most dioceses will emphasize the importance of the CME programme and meeting with peers. The bishop usually requires this to take priority over all parish activity, except in rare and serious circumstances such as the funeral of a churchwarden. Nevertheless the requirement needs to be acknowledged by both incumbent and curate, and included in the agreement.

Time for extra-parish placements, for involvement in the community, and with diocesan, national church or world church issues, and the expectations of working partners about these, should also be included. The specific issue of placements is dealt with more fully in the next chapter. It is helpful to incumbents to know what the curate is committing to outside the parish and it would be usual to specify that the agreement of the incumbent should be sought before extra-parochial ministry is undertaken.

Working time and time off

This may be a difficult area to explore together because some will assume that a priest is 'never off duty'; and in a sense we would agree. Yet some incumbents massively overwork and a clear idea of how much time, and when, the curate spends in active ministry is important to avoid frustration and painful conflict. Both the entry into professional ministry from a former career and also shifting cultural expectations have introduced changes in recent years. It is not unknown for training incumbents to be shocked by a curate's opening gambit, 'So, how many sessions do you want me to work a week?' Because it is a difficult area to discuss, it is essential that agreement is reached by each pair after clarifying their expectations.

It is impossible to quantify public ministry narrowly in terms of hours worked. If a session is thought of as a morning, afternoon or evening the conversation might become manageable. What is appropriate will vary, because the curate's circumstances and previous experience, and the ideas of the incumbent will vary in every situation. Which day off to have, and whether both take the same day will depend on assumptions about ministry styles. Hyperactive incumbents should make clear to the curate, 'Don't do what I do, but you must do what I tell you!' It is an improvement in ministry earnestly to be hoped for that a conversation about the working and time-off balance will result in the revision of an overworking incumbent's balance. In this respect we emphasize again the question posed in Chapter 1 – what ministry are you going to give up so that you have time for the supervision of a colleague?

Some simple guidance can be offered – a stipendiary curate working three sessions for five days a week (i.e. has a day off and only 'works' on Sunday in connection with services) is working too much. Clear expectations in the case of part-time, non-stipendiary minister (NSM) curates are extremely important lest they feel that more is asked than they are prepared to offer, or feel that advantage is being taken of them, or their willingness is being abused. An incumbent supporting a part-time NSM curate in saying no when appropriate will be offering them a great service.

Possibly incumbents can best help by protecting all curates from the excesses of the curate's own enthusiasm and from the insatiable demands of parish ministry.

Review

The working agreement should specify a date when it will be reviewed. Every three months is suggested, especially in the first year. This relieves both parties from the risk of anxiety about how and when to raise something. At the review what has been agreed should be examined briefly clause by clause to ensure both parties are happy with it. The contract or working agreement is not a legal document. It clarifies the expectations each has of the other and allows for modification as experience requires.

The topics offered here are not exhaustive but are intended to encourage thought, discussion and agreement in the process of contracting to work and learn together.

A clear contract or working agreement which includes expectations on all these and other items will prevent others suffering the frustration of the curate who wrote: 'I learned a lot, but it was by being left to do the job and find out on the spot by myself . . . I frequently felt unsupported, taken advantage of and discouraged.' It is highly doubtful that this pair had contracted successfully together, or that the incumbent had honoured it. Failure to contract can lead to confusion and misunderstanding, and further considerations are offered in Chapter 12. The failure can also lead to an abuse of power on the part of incumbents.

The supervision session

Time for supervision

Supervision is a precious resource for ministry, to be protected at all costs, and regularity is an important factor in the way supervision is used. The temptation is always there for supervision to be subordinated to other demands and to be postponed. There will be emergencies of course but regular changes of dates or cancellations of supervision sessions will lead to the belief that the need to review, reflect and learn in this crucial phase of ministry is not important. Supervision is crucial for its effect on future ministry. It is the place and the time that the new minister knows belongs to him or her, a reliable place where he or she can seek help and advice in a new, sometimes puzzling, demanding and sometimes stressful ministry. Supervision can be a safe haven, rather than a chore. With a clear structure for supervision a curate will be better able to take risks and try out new ideas.

A supervision session doesn't just happen. It needs to be planned and organized. Planned – part of a sequence of regular meetings: organized – in terms of what happens in the meeting. Most of us like to know 'where we are'. We are more comfortable, more open to take risks, more hopeful about the future when we know what will happen and when. For example, most of us are less anxious when we have found our seat in the train or plane, and even less anxious when we have sat in it for a bit and become familiar with our surroundings.

Agreement about supervision

The framework within which supervision sessions with the curate are conducted should also be specified in the working agreement.

Highlighted here are a number of areas that supervisor and curate should discuss together. They should clarify the assumptions and come to an agreement about each. Items should be expressed in the working agreement signed by both. This may seem very formal and a bit 'heavy' where two colleagues are working together in mutual trust and respect. The point is that contracting together what should and will happen is a major part of building that mutual trust and respect. It also protects each person when there is disagreement, and provides a framework for resolving conflict.

Confidentiality, secrecy and privacy

In spite of similarities between these terms, there is a difference between privacy, secrecy and confidentiality. Everyone has the right to *privacy* but privacy is about the right not to be interrupted in a supervision discussion as well as keeping things private between the supervisor and supervisee. The boundaries round our individual humanity and respect for our responsibility for ourselves require privacy to be acknowledged and protected in supervision.

Secrecy is a process in which information is acquired about people with no intention of sharing it with them. In this situation secrecy is rarely to be encouraged because it usually involves a manipulation of power over people. 'I am telling you this, but you must keep it secret', gives power to the sharer of information not only over the content of the 'secret', but also over the person to whom it is imparted. If something cannot be spoken of openly in supervision it is probably best kept to ourselves, except in extreme and very rare cases. Promises of secrecy are rarely reliable; as time goes by we all lose the details about what was spoken to us in secret, and what was not, and to whom we gave a promise not to pass it on.

Confidentiality is different. As a general principle the supervision process should be regarded as confidential between supervisor, supervisee and also to CME adviser and bishop's staff. For the most part confidences arising from the curate's work do not need to be communicated outside the supervision interview. However matters which have a wider significance for ministry, development and future work will need to be discussed with those outside the parish.

What a curate shares in supervision must normally be regarded as confidential. But in the supervisory situation confidentiality is never absolute. Information is gathered or acquired about people in order that they can receive feedback if they need it and use the information to good purpose and constructively. Both 'secret' and confidential work should be supervised. Effective supervision does not rely on people being identified in each and every situation. Supervision itself should be a confidential process, but never a secret one.

Concerning confidential conversations some good advice was offered by Southwell diocese as to how conversations on confidential matters should be conducted. The advice offers four important questions to be addressed:

What do we need to know?

There are many things about a situation or person we might or could know. It is tempting to want to know all there is, but probably unhelpful or invasive. Supervisor and supervisee will need to be clear which boundaries need to be crossed, and which boundaries are not crossed, even randomly or accidentally.

Why do we need to know?

It is a useful caution for a supervisor to be constantly asking either aloud, or to herself, 'Why do I need to know this?' in order to avoid wandering over the ground too widely or veering away from the central issues. A person discussing their feelings towards another person may well disclose a good deal of personal and sensitive information, which obviously must be treated with respect.

Do I need this information to check out my own feelings/behaviour or someone else's?

A supervisor needs to be self-aware and to avoid the temptation to curiosity or voyeurism. I may for instance talk about my private dealings with another to a third party because I am uncertain about my own response or because of something the other is doing. Whether my questions in supervision are for the curate's benefit or for my own is an important consideration in our face-to-face encounters.

How do we discuss it?

It is important to clarify at the start of what is going to be a confidential discussion where we hope to be at the end of it. This is especially important in more casual conversations. 'Let's bring this up in supervision' could be an appropriate response. If the matter is urgent then agreeing openly rather than making assumptions about confidentiality is important before the conversation ends. It also needs to be recognized that some participants in a conversation may be bound by externally applied conventions of confidentiality that do not bind others.

Agenda setting

Who is allowed to bring what to the supervision session? We have said enough already for it to be clear that this supervision time is primarily for the curate's learning about ministry. In Chapter 3 we discussed useful questions for supervisors to ask in order to help curates explore an issue. It should be clarified in the contract that both parties will avoid seeing the session as a convenient hybrid of different kinds of meetings happening at the same time, of work allocation and parish problem-solving. It should clarify that the agenda will be largely the curate's though that doesn't rule out the incumbent initiating something occasionally.

Agreement needs to be reached about the balance of input – how much is it the responsibility of the curate to bring work issues to supervision and how far it is possible for the incumbent to raise issues. A useful general assumption would be that 80/20 in the curate's favour should be about right. It is recognized that it is difficult to quantify these things. Nevertheless indicating a rough ratio that feels right provides for either person to raise the issue of balance in review if it is felt that the input is becoming unbalanced. Some notion of what was expected earlier will be very helpful when this happens.

Agreements about timing are also relevant here. A supervisor will be chary of dealing with last-minute items in a session. If a curate says it cannot wait then a warning bell should ring. The curate may be asking the incumbent to move into a different role, for example counsellor. Attending to last-minute items which extend the supervision time or are squeezed in at the end should be resisted.

Personal/spiritual boundaries in supervision

The question about how far incumbents feel they are concerned with a curate's spiritual development and formation must be examined. There will be different views. It needs to be agreed how far this does or does not come up in supervision. We suggest that it is a reasonable part of the incumbent's responsibility to ask whether the curate has an external guide for the spiritual life and whether the curate has met with the personal adviser provided by the diocese (where this is diocesan policy).

Should a couple pray together during the supervision sessions? No one would want to suggest that it is unwise to commend thinking, listening and speaking to the guidance of the Holy Spirit as you meet, or that outcomes and decisions should be offered in prayer so that they accord with God's will at the close. No advice is given here except to say that it is one of the issues about supervision that needs to be agreed between you.

Reporting on the progress, the entry into public ministry, the achievement of learning goals and development plans is a clear part of the incumbent's responsibility to the bishop and to the curate in the Anglican Church. The final report from college will help to form the conversation about learning goals in the first year because it is highly likely to contain areas for growth identified by the tutor and student together.

In the way of things this report is often general in nature and it is always worth asking a curate 'Is there anything that is not in the report that you think I should know?' There have been occasions where important information about curates was not made available to the incumbent. Knowledge about a curate's personal health or history might have helped to avoid stressful situations which contributed to future difficulties in the relationship. Incumbent and curate may need to find a way of talking about personal things that are going to be relevant for ministry.

The bishop may require a report before agreeing to ordination to the priesthood and may require annual reports usually from both curate and incumbent on the progress of the curate, and any items of concern. Guidance to incumbents on how to create such a report is usually provided by the diocese and facilitated by the CME officer. The important point here is that the report should be shared with the curate.

It may be helpful but it is not necessary that the curate is asked to agree with it. If there are genuine grounds for disagreement between incumbent and curate these need to be registered in the report. Curates and incumbents should not strive to produce an agreed form of words which may disguise different opinions or assessments. Nor should they engage in 'trade-offs' where information is suppressed in the interests of a compromise report. In fact many fruitful conversations at diocesan level have resulted from different views between an incumbent and curate about an item in the report. However it is part of good practice in the openness of supervision that the curate should read the report and be asked to sign it, whether or not this is required by the diocese.

When would it be right to report on a curate without the curate's assent or knowledge? If confidentiality is never absolute there may be extreme cases where the protection of the vulnerable, or care for the curate (for example in a case of serious illness or incapacity, or a significant domestic crisis), means the supervisor will want to pass on information without the consent of the curate. These cases will be extremely rare, but when they arise it would an abdication of responsibility for the supervisor not to act. Nevertheless she or he should always act as a last resort and after strenuous and sustained effort to persuade the curate to make a report for himself or herself. If the persuasion is successful it would be difficult to imagine a situation where the incumbent subsequently would not be asked for a report or to comment. In rare cases when a report is made without consent the person reported on should always be told that this has happened.

The guiding principle is to maximize openness. It should be clear to supervisor and supervisee that the one who has heard or observed another is handing back what has been observed, in order to allow the other to know what has been observed and to act upon it. To do this appropriately the information must be offered in ways which enable the other person to accept it, and not as accusations or condemnations.

This chapter has looked at the immediate practicalities of beginning to work with a curate. The next chapter will consider issues and problems that may arise for either you or your curate as you continue in your relationship.

Points for reflection

- When is the best time to produce a contract or working agreement?
- Have you indicated to the curate the areas to be included and given him or her time to think about it?
- If a copy is to be sent to the diocese is there a deadline? Are you aware of this date?
- How many discussions would it right to take to prepare a contract?
- Would it be right for each person separately to draft areas for discussion before a final draft is discussed?

9

Keeping it going

- Supervision only works if both parties are committed to it; are you both committed?
- Does your colleague raise any complaints or questions about the process of supervision?
- Are you able to fulfil your own expectations as a supervisor with your current workload?

In the last chapter we looked at starting work together, clarifying expectations and setting up a supervision programme. This chapter will explore how you continue on the journey. The focus of this chapter is maintaining the training relationship for the next three or four years when inevitably there will be tensions, and problems may arise.

There is a certain amount of chemistry in relationships and it isn't always obvious why some work well and others do not. Some general thoughts first provide a backdrop.

Authority

What makes the relationship of supervision distinctive is the power and authority vested in the incumbent, not only in relation to all the ministry of the parish but also in relation to the training of the newly ordained person. It is a compulsory relationship that each chose at a time when they had limited knowledge of each other and when external factors impinged on them from the diocese. Although it is to be hoped that contracting and negotiating a working agreement was trouble-free, the relationship will change and develop and situations will arise that were not anticipated at the outset.

Consider the story of one curate in the example below.

EXAMPLE 9.1 A female curate tells about eucharistic presidency

When her incumbent was presiding at the Parish Eucharist he naturally expected her to robe and walk just in front of him in procession even if she had no active role in the service. When she was presiding he always insisted on walking last in the procession and his curate had to walk in front of him wearing the chasuble. The curate had never seen this done in any other parish.

- What would you have done if you had been the incumbent, or the curate?
- What do you think is being symbolized by this attitude on the part of the incumbent?
- What issues of authority do you think it raises?
- What messages are conveyed to the congregation, and curate?

The distinctive authority of a priest to preach the Word and minister the sacraments is conveyed at ordination. The oversight of parish ministry and management is conveyed to an incumbent at institution and induction. In connection with authority in ministry we note that the morning after being ordained priest the curate has the same priestly authority as the incumbent. Nevertheless there will be a difference between them of confidence and experience and thus how each operates is likely to be different. A simple example will illustrate the point: in almost all dioceses curates are instructed by the bishop not to hear sacramental confessions until they have received instruction and been in priest's orders for at least two years.

Here is another story to show the difference between the two sorts of authority in the church. A curate and incumbent made a presentation on how they worked together at a training day. They told of how the vicar had been on holiday and a situation arose which involved the suspension or resignation of the organist. The curate was the only minister in the parish. The presentation showed what the curate did, and did not do, and how her actions were supported when the incumbent returned.

The details of what happened are not important. It is sufficient to say that the curate offered advice and support and pastoral care, while the matter of discipline and employment was handled by the churchwardens. The curate ministered with a priestly authority but made no attempt to usurp the authority of the incumbent, even though he was absent. The curate ceased to have any continuing involvement in the situation when the incumbent returned, when the continuing situation was managed by the incumbent and churchwardens acting together. The incumbent publicly supported and endorsed what the curate had done. This was a clear example of appropriate role behaviour in a difficult situation.

Here each had equivalent authority by virtue of ordination, yet the curate had no authority over the organist except concerning the conduct of public worship for the duration of the time she was presiding. Not all situations are as clear-cut as this. Being clear about the difference between the authority for priestly ministry and oversight for the whole parish is important so that wires are not crossed and everyone understands who holds the boundaries round processes of work and ministry.

One of the goals of the first few years is that the curate should learn to handle her or his own authority as a minister of the gospel, and to accept with maturity that he or she works under authority. This will mean extensive opportunities to exercise ministerial authority, and reviewing feelings, attitudes and the processes associated with that authority.

Some curates may need opportunities to develop skills associated with incumbency towards the end of their first post. An incumbent may want a curate to experience chairing a PCC, especially if the curate has little experience of chairing groups and formal committees before ordination. Technically, an incumbent is required to occupy the chair at the PCC by virtue of office, but a training situation might create an acceptable deviation. It might be undesirable for the incumbent to manufacture an absence and to invite the curate to chair on that occasion, even if the prior agreement of the lay chair is secured. An incumbent will probably want to be present at the meeting a curate is invited to chair. Even if he or she decides to take no active part in the meeting, effective feedback based on first-hand knowledge can then be offered in supervision.

This is not an exhaustive treatment of issues of authority in the Church. It serves to illustrate some of the concerns relevant in training.

Friendship

It is good when Christian ministers, working together, can be friends as well as working colleagues but it is not required for good training. *Friends* is to be distinguished from *friendly*. Becoming friends can imply a certain mutuality and equality in the relationship which may deny the reality of power and authority. The relationship may become more difficult when power and authority are ignored and when each finds it difficult to say things to the other that arise from that reality. But friendliness is an entirely appropriate characteristic. Not only do we testify to the many friendly relationships between incumbents and curates which are very effective and healthy, but it is difficult to imagine a good relationship in which friendliness does not play a useful part.

Nevertheless friendliness is not *necessary* in the way that mutual trust and respect are, and it carries some dangers in the background. Burgess (1998) describes some dysfunctional relationships where curates describe over-friendly relations as unhelpful and even oppressive.

There should be friendly relations between incumbent and newly ordained, and this will make for good training and ministry with others. But it is important to maintain clarity both of purpose and task, for example between staff meetings, supervision sessions and social occasions. The reality of accountability and authority that goes with the training relationship should not be compromised, even if incumbents and curates expect to be friendly towards each other. The example from the last chapter of the incumbent and curate meeting to do supervision in the pub should be a cautionary tale. An age gap between an older curate and a younger incumbent should not be allowed to undermine the authority of the incumbent and the reporting structures. Open friendly relations are good and laudable, but supervisor and supervisee should be very cautious about meeting their emotional needs for close friendship with each other rather than other people.

Placements and projects

It is important that curates have an opportunity both to use their gifts and to learn in the community, the diocese and the wider Church. This may be in the form of a chaplaincy or membership of a national association or involvement in diocesan structures. It is unlikely that this will be significant in the first year since there will be much else that will need to be learned, and establishing the main work-base in the parish will be important. Nevertheless as wide a range of experience in the first post as is appropriate will help to build the ministry of the future.

A pair of contemporary stipendiary curates work-shadowed each other alternately for two weeks each. Their social contexts were very different and there was much learning about models of ministry that arose for each. One of them said: 'It was just the right time because I was beginning to sharpen up in my mind what sort of next parish I was looking for.' She said also:

> I hadn't anticipated the opportunity to observe the relationship of the training incumbent and curate in the other parish. As I watched the way they related to one another I was able to reflect on my own relationship with my training incumbent and this helped me think through the dynamics of how we worked. I also appreciated seeing how a different style of incumbent works and it enabled me to explore my own ways of working.

Examples of useful and successful placements undertaken by curates in the experience of the authors have been

- Short-term hospital chaplaincy
- Secondment for part of the week for a period to a local prison chaplaincy
- Placement with the Mission in the World of Work team
- An exchange between a curate in an affluent suburb and a curate in a UPA parish for three weeks.

Apart from a different context an advantage of placement in a different parish is the opportunity provided to observe another model of incumbency and to contrast it with that of the training incumbent, and even perhaps share another experience of supervision where one curate work-shadows another.

Examples of some projects undertaken by curates have been

- Management of the development of a community centre in the parish
- Setting up and leading an Asian girls/women's football team
- Writing a higher education textbook on nuclear physics
- Attachment to a religious broadcaster and communications officer
- Research project on contemporary adult spirituality.

Agreement should be reached about how much time should be allowed for extra-parochial experience and responsibility. It would be the continuing responsibility of the incumbent to provide supervision during and after the placement and/or project unless other arrangements are made with someone with specialist knowledge.

A cautionary note might be useful here. Curates are often seen, not unreasonably, as a bonus for the deanery, and while encouraging the acquisition of wide experience an incumbent will be wise to exercise a critical judgement about the number of wider activities that come the curate's way. The priority of the first post is a learning framework. It is a precious resource that will never come again. The wise incumbent will want to be sure that a multitude of experiences is not substituted for depth of learning, even if this involves a certain amount of unpopularity with colleagues, or even the curate!

Apart from placements there is the issue of acquiring basic learning experiences when opportunities are not available in the parish. Another story from the case of the rural curate mentioned in the previous chapter is instructive. There were few funerals in the scattered hamlets in the benefice, and generally families wanted and expected the popular and long-serving incumbent to conduct them. This meant that the curate didn't take his first funeral until well into his second year. He felt disadvantaged in the year group of curates because he had nothing to share from his experience with his peers. It was suggested that opportunities to take a funeral in a nearby town could have been provided. Again, he felt this was undesirable because he felt more unsure than others in his year group of his developing skills. Another effect of the way service-leading was arranged was that he hardly ever had an opportunity to observe the incumbent, nor the incumbent to observe him on Sundays. It would help if cover from retired or unbeneficed clergy was sought as eventually happened in this story. The principle of seeking experience in other parishes that cannot be found in the home parish not only holds true for rural curates, but could be important for all curacies.

Using a work consultant

At the heart of supervision is the idea of sitting with someone and reflecting together on ministry, as it is actually delivered and how it is felt. This is provided for new ministers in the supervisory relationship, but this is something that all ministers do well to search out for themselves. Many dioceses provide networks of work consultants so that skilled and experienced people are available to ministers to help them reflect on their ministry and grow and develop through it. The busier a training incumbent is the more she or he might value meeting periodically with an external consultant.

Often spiritual directors, work consultants or mentors, and counsellors are mentioned in the same breath, but there are careful distinctions to be made between them. There is often a great area of common concern and overlap and at the same time it is helpful to see how they are different. This difference is best thought of as different focus. The spiritual direction conversation keeps the focus on the minister's relationship with God; the counsellor keeps the focus on the person; and the work consultant keeps the focus on the being and doing ministry. All three have their time and place and value, and a minister without any of these is often on a path towards burnout or dysfunction.

Training and coaching styles – moving 'hands on' to 'hands off'

Supervision sessions are always going to be important for those whose professional life involves working with people, including clergy. The supervision provided by an incumbent for a curate will continue throughout the first post. However the coaching, training or mentoring style of the incumbent as he guides a colleague into professional ministerial norms of ministry is going to evolve during the time they work together. The how-to-do-it knowledge that a curate needs will involve much more hands-on training and coaching from the incumbent in the first months and year. The guidance offered and the depth of coaching required will be more advisory as the curacy proceeds. Eric Parsloe (1999) offers a diagram to describe how the partners move in relation to each other as the professional coaching relationship matures (see Figure 9.1).

An incumbent will find the degree of control she or he has reducing in favour of the curate as time proceeds (Figure 9.1). Two points are worth noting. You will see that the diagonal lines do not quite join the lower corners indicating that at no point does either incumbent or curate have absolute control; there is always the willing involvement of the other to be taken into account.

The second point is that the model describes an overall style. Yet the colleagues are likely to be in different places and require different sorts of coaching over different issues at the same moment in the curacy. For example a curate with considerable experience of conducting funerals as a reader or lay minister will not need hands-on coaching about taking funerals after ordination, but will need considerable guidance about conducting marriages. Similarly a curate with significant experience of chairing meetings in business and commercial life will need only hands-off coaching with regard to knowing the

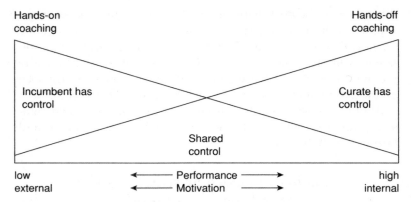

Figure 9.1 Coaching styles continuum – a 'midwife' model

This material is adapted from *The Manager as Coach and Mentor 2nd ed.*, by Eric Parsloe (1999), with the permission of the publisher, the Chartered Institute of Personnel and Development, London.

legalities of, say, the Church Council, but may need guidance in developing a different leadership style with volunteers.

An exercise that an incumbent and curate might do together is to mark separately on Figure 9.1 where they think they are at the end of a period, perhaps every six months or year. Comparing the results together could lead to fruitful conversations about needs and expectations concerning the training issues under review.

Looking ahead

How far ahead should a training incumbent look as she or he guides the colleague in these crucial early years? The bishop may expect a yearly review from both of progress and achievements. This may include setting goals for learning in the next year.

A curacy will usually last three years or four years. Three is the minimum but there are exceptions when curates leave for greater responsibility earlier. Short-term thinking will be more natural in the first year, but as you get to know your colleague and her or his natural strengths and any shortcomings, it will be useful to have a sense of how your curate's vocation might play out. All options will usually be open until at least the end of the third year. Nevertheless some idea of what kind of ministry he or she expects next will prompt the offering of certain experiences and allow for creating opportunities designed to maximize the training.

A stipendiary curate will be looking for another stipendiary post. If your colleague is not stipendiary what level of leadership will be suitable, and how much time will he or she be able to give to it? The range of options is more fluid now. Would an NSM curate expect to continue as a colleague with another incumbent? Might he be offered, or look for, a post as priest-in-charge? An NSM priest-in-charge will offer the sort of leadership that parallels incumbency and will need preparing for it in a way that a continuing curacy will not need.

Devolving areas of responsibility and creating leadership opportunities for a colleague will involve a conversation probably in the year after ordination as priest. Because parish ministry is a generic ministry it is important for the newly ordained to have a wide experience in the same way that a newly qualified doctor will need experience in a wide range of medical problems with a wide range of people. This could be frustrating for a specialist curate, and we deal with specialist ministries in Chapter 13. It is not a good idea for a former youth worker to have responsibility for developing youth ministry in a first post no matter how opportunistic it may seem. The curate's holistic development should predominate – which is not to say that previous experience will not suggest that someone might act as consultant or adviser to others who lead in that area. In delegating a role or responsibility to a curate an incumbent will delegate the authority as well and make it clear that this has happened. It may be a training post, but everyone should be clear that the curate is exercising real ministry. Delegation in this context means that the incumbent will be very cautious about allowing bypass or appeals to herself from people with whom the curate is working. Mutual trust and respect should be the keynotes of the delegation, and should be obvious to others.

Finally, it is not easy to lay down guidance on how far ahead an incumbent should look. The focal length will be more concentrated and increasingly short-term as the curacy progresses.

The focus of this chapter has been the more usual issues that arise in supervision within working relationships once colleagues are working together. The next chapter returns to the more direct theme of facilitating learning – by enabling goals to be set and learning to be recorded.

Points for reflection

- What skills, knowledge, values and attitudes in your current ministry as supervisor can you affirm and celebrate from reading this chapter?
- Consider one specific and achievable change you want to make in supervision as a result of reading this chapter.
- Would you welcome a meeting for mutual support, the sharing of problems and solutions for training incumbents in your year group?
- If this is not organized/supported by the diocese, could you take the initiative with your colleagues?
- What sort of placement opportunities might there be for a curate in your local community, your deanery and the diocese?

10

Setting learning goals and recording learning

- Do you think identifying learning goals is useful?
- How useful is it to record what you learn?
- If you agree that it is, how do you help someone to do it?

The importance of setting goals

Unless you know what you want to learn, and in what order, your learning will be haphazard and at the mercy of events. It would be important to learn how to use a saw, hammer and screwdriver before learning how to replace your skirting board, to take an obvious example. A ministerial life without vision is aimless and likely to be drifting. Goals are simply steps on the way to achieve your vision. We often let ourselves drift down the stream, guided by chance, or what we believe to be chance, reacting as situations arise. We can justify this approach by appealing to the necessity to be responsive to what God reveals to us in the moment. But God's vision for his Kingdom does not depend on chance. Unless you set goals you are not giving proper value to his call to you to be part of the Body building his Kingdom. So whatever our psychological preference might be, a sense of setting out on a journey with things to be achieved is crucial to an effective ministry. The Church has identified what it requires of those being ordained in terms of those qualities, understanding and skills it needs for those in positions of authority and leadership. These are expressed as learning outcomes.

It will be clear from some of the ideas about psychological type (see Chapter 5) that different people will approach the question of setting goals in different ways. One person will be more open and spontaneous and might say: 'I'm learning all the time, I prefer to investigate things as they come along. I'd rather reflect when the opportunity arises.' Another will be more ordered and structured and might say: 'I want to know what the syllabus is, and to finish this project before I start on another. Let's plan a schedule for learning.' But while we might have a preference, we are not prevented by that preference from acting in another way.

The Church of England has had goals for learning in the first years of ministry for a long time. These were first formally articulated by the Advisory Board for Ministry in *Beginning Public Ministry – the First Four Years* (January 1998). In recent years there has been a significant change in the integration of learning for ministry and a clearer expression of goals that takes place before ordination, after it and continuing throughout active ministry. The current learning outcomes for ordained ministry in relation to these phases can be found in *Formation for Ministry within a Learning Church* on the Ministry Division's website <www.cofe-ministry.org.uk>. Education and training for ministry is much more clearly seen as a continuum consisting of related phases, both pre- and post-ordination initial ministerial education (IME), and ongoing ministry. This education will include a rigorous assessment of knowledge, skills, character, spirituality and integrity at various key points at the appropriate time.

Most Church of England dioceses require a report to the bishop from both curate and supervising incumbent at the end of each year of ministry assessing what has been learned both in terms of quality as well as range. The report is likely to include learning outcomes for the coming year.

In setting the learning outcomes, four areas of concern should inform the identification of the learning pathway. The national learning outcomes for IME for Anglicans and Methodists are provided in section two of the Archbishops' Council's document *Formation for Ministry in a Learning Church*. There will be previous experience and learning that a curate brings. There will be personal learning needs of which a curate is aware following the review of the pre-ordination learning. There is also learning for ministry that the parish context requires in order for the curate to be an effective local minister. Thus out of a discussion involving the curate, the incumbent and the diocesan CME adviser or tutor will emerge the goals for each year of a curate's ministry.

The Church of England has identified minimum expectations of the time to be allocated for learning in the first few years. In summary this is expressed as 40 days per year (13 per cent of ministerial time), for full-time ministers. For 'part-time' ministers, learning time should be seen as something like 20 evenings per year plus one five-day residential and three study days. Some of this learning will be acquired in peer groups, some in one-to-one tutoring, some may be continuing in an academic environment, some with the incumbent in the parish. There could also be placements and secondments for the achievement of specific learning goals.

Learning contracts

Apart from the identification of yearly learning outcomes there may be academic study that a curate wishes to pursue for personal development. Generally speaking there is likely to be a considerable amount of time for learning occupying curates in the first years of ministry. Together with the transition into a role in a new parish, academic study should be undertaken cautiously and only after the new situation has been properly assessed. Nevertheless there are situations where this would be entirely appropriate.

During his stipendiary curacy a formerly employed scientist and adviser not only wrote a university course textbook in nuclear physics but also contributed articles and lectures on the relationship between cosmology and theology.

In these cases it would be good practice for a contract to be made between the curate and the incumbent. While primarily being a contract between the two of them with the agreement of the diocese, it is necessary to guard against a tendency for one party to manipulate the other. This contract should be written and indicate what area is to be studied, whether an academic award is sought, the duration of the course and what work is expected to be covered in a year. The contract should be dated and signed by the incumbent.

Recording learning

Jennifer Moon (1999) describes the importance of the ability to express or represent learning. Sometimes, of course, this is necessary to satisfy external requirements – to pass an examination, to satisfy a teacher, to acquire a qualification – but it is also necessary for the individual learner. Unless he or she can express the learning, that learning is not complete. Representing learning in the form of an essay, report or in conversation offers the individual the opportunity to reflect again and to make new discoveries. In this way a learner can extend and deepen the benefits acquired from the experience and progress further.

For many people, verbal methods are often the most usual and most comfortable ways to express and record learning. Some of the ways this can be done are:

- Note-taking
- Journaling
- Reflective diary
- A piece of critical writing
- Devising an imaginative scenario
- Writing up a project
- Workshop or course programme with simple commentary
- Book reviews or a summary of reading
- Ministry audit.

Poetry, as well as drawing, painting, model-making and other non-verbal methods could also be helpful.

Where significant personal learning has taken place, especially when changes in perception have taken place, verbal methods might be introduced with some sentences such as the following:

- I now see that my past opinions were influenced by stereotypes. Now I am approaching the situation differently.
- My outlook has developed since . . . I am critical of what we are trying to do. Let me explain how.
- I used to justify things by approaching them pragmatically. Now I approach things more on the basis of principle.

Adults like to relate learning to what they already know and to their life experience. For example a number of adults were attending an A-level course in sociology which was composed mainly of teenagers. They kept wanting to stop the tutor to discuss how they related to sociological concepts of referent groups (people they identified with), social mobility (how they had changed from their parents), and education (how they choose schools for their children). This was not always appreciated by the younger members of the class who were more focused on passing the examination! Training incumbents may like to ask, in different ways, the question, 'How does this look to you now that you are ordained?' as a way of helping curates to record the changes in the way they regard previous experience or their experience at theological college or course.

A critical moment when significant learning is triggered might be recorded by a curate.

EXAMPLE **10.1 Notes about a funeral which went particularly well or which had problems**

1 The experience – the story and context of the experience is recorded succinctly.
2 This is what I did – the options I had and why I chose to act as I did
3 What I learnt from this
4 What I might do differently in the future
5 Further questions I am left with

Appendix 6 offers a model for recording used by one curate in which comments by the incumbent could be made. More can be found in using the process of critical incident analysis in ministry in the Grove Booklet, *Growing in Ministry: Using Critical Incident Analysis* by C. Chadwick and P. Tovey.

A simple but highly effective method of recording not only the experience of learning but also the effect of the learning would be to divide a page into two columns. In one column the processes of a learning experience are recorded and opposite them in the second column the views and feelings are noted in connection with each. This was a very useful process used by one curate over a significant piece of ministry requiring interactions over an extended period. The curate recorded any views or comment which had been offered by her training incumbent. Every now and again a short paragraph was written across both columns which began with 'What I have learned by reflecting on the previous section'.

Another curate kept a journal about learning to celebrate at 1662 Holy Communion, a service with which she had not been familiar until ordination. She noted what she did on the first occasions, what surprised her and what mistakes she made, and went back to it on subsequent occasions and added further comments. In this way she produced an overview of her learning and development over a period which she found affirming and confidence-building.

Oxford diocese pioneered the competencies for ministry and suggestions as to how people might offer evidence that they had fulfilled the requirements under each heading within an area of learning. These were called *Gifts and Competencies* (updated annually). For example, following the theme of funeral ministry, the requirement in the *Gifts and Competencies for Planning and Leading Worship – Funerals* expected that people would provide evidence that:

1 They knew about death, loss and bereavement;
2 They were ministering to bereaved people;
3 They knew about preparing for the funeral service;
4 They could conduct and/or assist at the service with sensitivity.

There are sophisticated complexities to the *Gifts and Competencies* involving ranges of experience (among which in this case were old age, suicide, euthanasia), and a series of levels indicating depth of knowledge and experience. These are not directly relevant to recording learning. It suffices to say that a systematic approach might encourage a curate to review and record learning holistically and to consider ways in which gaps might be addressed in the future. Coventry diocese encouraged curates to write their own gifts and competencies with the encouragement and expertise of year-group tutors, and to produce evidence in relation to each with the collaboration of training incumbents. More ideas could be developed by looking again at Chapter 6 – 'Reflection: what it is and how to do it'.

Ideas for keeping learning going by enabling curates to be deliberate in their learning and to recognize their achievements have been offered in this chapter. The next one explores some more specific problems that may arise for both supervisor and supervisee.

Points for reflection

- How do you know what you have learned?
- Do you rely on your intuition and memory or do you prefer to keep some sort of learning log?
- If you were applying for another post how might you show what you had learned about ministry and yourself in your current post?

11

Problems you might encounter

- Do you avoid supervision sessions with those for whom you have oversight or do you look forward to them?
- Do you find supervision difficult or easy?
- Do you think conflict is a necessary part of human life and is the way we sort priorities and make decisions?
- Do you on the other hand ignore, deny or minimize conflict?
- If you have a curate in post already, or previously, what problems have you encountered?

Boundaries of person and role

Before we examine specific problems there is a general topic to be addressed concerning the limitations of the training incumbent's responsibility, and this is a good place to deal with it. The question was asked by training incumbents in a preparation meeting, 'Since the pastoral care of all who live in the parish is a key part of my ministry and responsibility, how far is the personal life of the curate, and his or her partner, my concern?'

It is a real question for all incumbents, and there is no simple answer. Of course you will care about the curate and his or her family. But you are also in an 'employer' role, to put it rather crudely, and you are accountable to the bishop for your curate's development and ability to take up significant leadership roles in the life of the Church. Your relationship with the curate mirrors, in some aspects, your bishop's relationship with you, at least so far as your expectations about care and pastoral matters might be concerned. You will probably expect the bishop and his staff to take an interest in your health and welfare, especially when there are difficulties. But you might not want him to get too close and to take too much of an interest since, to some degree, opportunities for future ministry might be in his hands.

There is a boundary between us as people who occupy a role and the integrity and privacy of the individual and their freedom under

God. Personal differences in ministry are always difficult boundary issues because who we are is at least as important as what we do. The boundary may be permeable, but it is a real one.

Read the case study in the example below and note how you would answer the questions there before reading on.

EXAMPLE 11.1 Boundaries of person and role – a case study

A married incumbent has a single curate, ordained deacon six months ago. The curate is living alone in a different part of the parish. It is mentioned to the incumbent (not necessarily critically) by a churchgoing parishioner that a person of different sex from the curate is seen leaving the house at breakfast time quite frequently and that this has been noticed by neighbours who are not churchgoers.

- What would you do if you were the incumbent?
- Would you raise the issue with the curate? And if so what would you say?
- What would you say to the parishioner who mentioned it to you?

How did you answer the questions in the box? Your answers will depend a lot on how you thought about the boundary between person and role. Different incumbents will have answered the questions in different ways. Some might feel grateful that they haven't had to deal with them in reality!

Perhaps you thought the lifestyle of the curate was not consonant with ordained ministry. If you did you may have found it more or less easy to know what to do or say to the curate, or for that matter to anyone else. How might you respond if the curate had said, 'It's none of your business so long as my work is satisfactory'? If you had shared your concern with the curate how might you have responded if the curate had said, 'It is all right for you, you've already found a partner. How do I find one? It is difficult living in a goldfish bowl!'

Maybe you thought it was no business of yours, in which case how would you respond to the parishioner, if at all? Maybe you would take a middle course and urge discretion on all concerned. Even if you do take a middle course the question will arise about whether you say anything in your report on the deacon's year to the bishop – and, if so, what?

This example illustrates the difficulties about the boundaries, particularly relevant for those in public ministry, about who we are, what others perceive of us, how we live our lives, and the ministerial work we do.

An important view holds that just because someone is working with you under supervision you do not have the right to know about personal issues and the private life of a curate, nor the right to probe for that knowledge in supervision, unless it obviously impinges on their ability to be a public minister and representative of the Church. The boundaries to be observed here concern the integrity and privacy of the individual and their walk with God. Supervision is not therapy or counselling and that boundary must be respected. If the work of the curate is satisfactory the incumbent must let other concerns rest there. Anything else could be experienced as intrusive or oppressive.

Burgess writes of a curate who felt her incumbent's question about what she did on her day off as inappropriate.

> I told him, 'I don't want you to ask me this, it's my day off; it's actually none of your business what I do' . . . It may have been a general concern (for me) . . . but it didn't *feel* like that; it felt intrusive. (Burgess, 1998)

Looking at another boundary, how should the incumbent relate pastorally to the curate's partner, if they have one? Pastoral care is a slightly easier matter here, but it is not necessarily straightforward. There may be a concern about a curate's partner; perhaps the incumbent notices that he or she stops attending church or looks ill or anxious. How should the incumbent respond? As the curate's 'boss' you are in a different relationship with the curate's partner – different from that with other members of the congregation. It would surely be right to enquire and express concern. It would be easy and would save time to enquire of the curate about the partner. Enquiring directly of the partner is probably better because in that way your pastoral role is less likely to be compromised by your relationship with the curate. Nevertheless the approach requires a delicacy and sensitivity to the boundaries involved. If you feel that this is not appropriate, the question as to who exercises pastoral care for the partner of a curate remains to be addressed.

It is a similar issue for a single curate who falls in love and starts to date someone in the parish. The curate is both a minister to that person and a potential partner. It is useful, and probably proper, for the curate to declare the romantic interest to the incumbent and formally hand over pastoral care of the potential partner to someone else in the ministry team. In this sense the curate is then free to pursue the relationship without at least some potential hindrances or complications coming between them.

At the end of the day we don't expect all who read this book will come to the conclusions that we have about boundaries between person and role. Nevertheless we each have our personal journey through life and our individual journey with God. While these inform and contribute to our ministry, and vice versa, the boundary between person and role deserves respect and must be crossed by the supervising incumbent reluctantly, with the right motivation, only in emergency and with great care.

Transference

This is not the place to deal adequately with psychodynamic systems, which need thorough and specialist treatment. Nevertheless it is important to recognize that there are processes of human interaction which are present in every relationship and can get in the way of effective supervision. This may be especially so where two people are working together in a partnership which is relatively private and not open to observation and inspection by other professionals. Transference occurs when someone projects, onto another person, emotions which were previously felt in some other relationship, for example with a parent. In this way a person is related to as if she or he were that other person. The process is very largely unconscious unless the individual becomes aware of it.

These aspects of transference often occur in relationships where there is a difference of power, age, sex or experience. All ministers soon learn that transference is something they have to be able to recognize and respond to, as members of the congregation and the public relate to them as authority, moral or religious figures. So transference is also likely to be part of the supervision relationship, both by the curate to the incumbent and by the incumbent to the curate.

It may be an issue about any personal difference. In an example, a curate complained that her incumbent treated her like a daughter, or an incumbent might say that his curate expected him to behave like a father, and reacted as if he was. The clue to transference – the importation into a relationship of powerful feelings which originate elsewhere – is the experience of feelings both from and towards the other person which on reflection seem to be out of place. Sometimes these feelings are expressed in behaviours or attitudes which can be a clue that transference is operating in the relationship. These feelings may create very uncomfortable feelings, especially if they are sexual or aggressive.

Apart from talking it through, incumbents and curates who suspect that transference is beginning to operate inappropriately in the relationship will probably need to articulate and to clarify their differences of opinion about the purpose of supervision. It will be necessary to voice the assumptions and unexpressed reactions they have to each other. If a situation involving transference becomes serious enough to make meeting difficult, outside help must be sought. We turn now to some of the specific problems and issues that might arise.

You say: '*I haven't got time to supervise my curate*'

It is as important to affirm what you are doing well, and what is going well in your joint ministry, as it is to tackle areas that need improving. Is it really a time issue, or one of confidence? Do you feel competent to deal with theological questions that might arise for someone who has finished academic theology more recently than you? Perhaps you feel incompetent in the skills you see as necessary for effective supervision?

If it is a question of theological confidence, you may be surprised at your own unacknowledged rationale for ministry once you are required to voice it. We all really know why things happen and have a theological framework within which we operate, but we often put ourselves down because thinking theologically may have become so much part of our second nature that we fail to recognize it for what it is. To improve your self-confidence when a question arises, buy yourself time for thinking about it. Say that you would like time to give a proper answer to the question when you have considered it. In that way you are less likely to feel under pressure.

If it is a question about confidence in your skills for the process of supervision you could seek help from an experienced training incumbent or the CME adviser or bring to a support group of training incumbents the question, 'What do you do if . . . ?' There are a lot of people out there who are only too willing to help, if you ask! You may also be voicing a concern that is felt by others.

Incumbents should avoid giving negative messages to themselves, 'It's all my fault', or projecting responsibility onto the curate, 'It's all her or his fault.' The modelling of supervision is important, not only for its own sake but because a good experience as a curate will encourage the colleague to seek that sort of help or work consultancy when they are self-managing and self-motivating in the future. In the long term it will be good experience to be drawn on when the curate supervises others. We belong within the Body of Christ and no one should be asked to minister in isolation in the Church. The confidence and ability to seek support at all stages in a ministerial career is crucial for effective ministry in a fast-changing world and Church.

If it really is a question of time then the supervisor needs to shed some responsibilities, perhaps only for the time being. Thus, space is created for proper supervision. This would be a good opportunity to develop lay leadership and offer others chances of growing in ministry. This is a matter of discernment and leadership. It would be tempting to delegate to others responsibilities that you don't enjoy or don't do well. That would be good if there is obviously someone who has the gifts and aptitude for it – in which case it is worth asking why you haven't delegated it before. In the long term it is more likely to be supportive and effective to delegate areas of responsibility where solid and respected foundations have been laid.

An incumbent might need to think this through with someone: work consultant? Spiritual adviser? Churchwardens? A good friend?

Curate says: '*I don't need supervision*'

Everyone who is in ministry needs supervision, and it will help if the incumbent can model this by being open about his or her own arrangements for supervision. The effective training incumbent will want to avoid colluding with this resistance to supervision and see this attitude as symptomatic. What is the real problem here? Perhaps it is fear of exposure, fear of examining failure or acknowledging inadequacy. Questions will need to dig deeper. What are the symptoms? The effects of failure are deadening and are revealed by a number of characteristic symptoms. Someone who is suffering from unexamined failure may show some or all of the following:

- Loss of interest in the issue/item
- Loss of confidence – thrown off course, disorientated
- Giving up more quickly in the future

- Reluctance to face new tasks: seeking to avoid change
- Reluctance to co-operate
- Expecting failure again
- Escaping from failure into daydreaming or depression
- Setting lower standards in the present and future.

If some or all of these are seen in the curate then an incumbent will need to find ways of building self-esteem. With someone in training this will need to be tackled head-on and immediately. It may help to offer undiluted praise. Find something that has gone really well and offer positive feedback. Perhaps encourage other people to do so as well. No one can have too much genuine praise for work well done.

The effects of success can be seen in the following list:

- Greater interest in the activity or topic
- Confidence grows – able readily to accept the occasional failure
- Persistence in the face of failure; goals are likely to grow
- Increased ability to co-operate
- Increased emotional control
- Tendency to revise goals.

Look for these signs in a specific piece of work and give really affirming feedback. Brief notes on how to give praise with maximum effect are included at Appendix 4.

An incumbent will find it is worth reflecting on whether it is anything that he or she might have done, even inadvertently, to produce this sense of failure. The more the ministers working with supervisors are involved in setting standards the more they will be committed to accepting them. Helping people in supervision is about creating a safe space where self-criticism can be encouraged, dialogue can be heard, risks taken, developments considered/planned, and experiments anticipated. Is there any way in which a supervisor may have communicated that this might not be true?

Perhaps it would be useful to look at a list originally offered as 'The Short Course in Leadership', attributed to John Adair:

The six most important words:	I admit I made a mistake
The five most important words:	May I offer you feedback?
The four most important words:	I'm proud of you
The three most important words:	What's your opinion?
The two most important words:	Thank you
The one most important word:	Please
The least important word:	I

However supervisors can too readily take on the blame for problems in supervision. At the end of the day it is a joint enterprise that requires equal commitment. Most people will respond positively to the message, 'I want you to be a good priest/minister. I know you can be. Let's see how we can achieve that together.' Try to avoid on the one hand taking on all the responsibility yourself, 'It's all my fault', or on the other projecting responsibility, 'It's all your fault'. It could be necessary to explore what attitudes and life experience contribute to such a defence against supervision. This may require external professional help.

Curate says: '*There's nothing to discuss*'

Reluctance to engage in a planned supervision session may result from an enhanced opinion of one's own abilities and competence. It may be a defensive reaction to the situation described in the section above. It may also be a product of overbusyness and a failure to prepare adequately. The attitude may show itself in seeking agreement not to meet, failing to turn up, or producing nothing for the meeting and sitting mostly in silence while expecting the colleague to initiate discussion. It is one of the games sometimes played in the supervision relationship and every supervisor will have experienced this at some time or other.

One reaction would be to say, 'This is your time, unless you bring an issue for us to look at we shall be wasting your time and mine' and then for the incumbent to sit in silence, but it risks producing more defensiveness. It would be tempting, and occasionally justified, to bring up something that the supervisor wants to discuss. If this is what is decided it would be well to make it absolutely clear that this is exceptional and that the colleague will be expected to initiate topics for review or discussion at the next meeting.

It would be better by far to anticipate the problem by the way supervision is set up from the start. A defined structure which has been agreed at the beginning will help to minimize the problem. In an hour-and-a-half session that might be agreed with a curate the time could normally be divided into three parts. The first ten or 15 minutes is spent reviewing any actions agreed or decisions made at the end of the previous session and examining a piece of work that has happened in the intervening period. The last ten minutes is to be spent preparing or planning for something that is coming up, and the middle period devoted to an extended discussion together about an aspect of ministry. Quite obviously, it would need to be flexible, and on occasions the review could lead into the major discussion if the matter is urgent and significant. At other times it might provide material for a future supervision session, especially if it is something for which either partner needs to prepare. Once a pattern similar to this has been established, the value of the sessions should be recognized. Signalling from the start that a piece of preparation needs to be seen some days before the meeting could also inhibit the nothing-to-discuss gambit. An example of a preparation sheet is given in Appendix 7.

It is worth a little self-examination again to reflect on whether it is something you have done or said that has raised defences unnecessarily. It is a key part of the incumbent's role to offer criticism. Has the incumbent been overcritical, or has a contribution or feedback been experienced as destructive rather than constructive? Simple guidance on offering criticism is given at Appendix 5.

Supervision of the sort described and advocated is not about just solving problems. Its purpose is rather to provide for the development of ministerial competence; to enable the curate to reflect on her or his interactions with parishioners and others they meet in the course of ministry; to examine others' expectations of them and their feelings about these expectations; and to create space for constructive feedback. This could mean reviewing any piece of work or aspect of ministry, not just difficulties. One question that might be asked in supervision might be: 'Could you tell me about something you have done, or something in which you are involved, about which you are continuing to think?' This would signal that it is not just problems that are appropriate here. It would also indicate that the items the supervisee has energy for are the ones that are best focused on in supervision.

Curate is blocked in the learning cycle

Either of the situations above where the curate appears reluctant to engage with you in supervision may be a result of getting blocked in the learning cycle described in Chapter 5, and thus learning becomes inhibited. We all have times like this when we are unable to move through the different stages of reflection, theorizing, and planning pragmatic action or learning through experience.

Usually someone will find it difficult to engage fully in an aspect of learning that he or she finds difficult or of which there is little previous experience; so it is important to notice which parts of the cycle seem to be skimped or quickly passed over. To ensure that the curate, and maybe you, become more effective learners it will be useful to practise in the areas in which you feel least at home.

There are times also when supervision seems difficult or slow because a learner gets blocked and seems to get stuck in one of the aspects of learning and is unable to move into the next phase. This can happen for a number of reasons, and the result is that learning is inhibited and ministry does not develop.

Tony Morrison offers some strategies in *Staff Supervision in Social Care* (1993), which he says will generally be in one of three areas: increasing awareness of feelings and experience, developing skills to think about and analyse situations in depth, and ways to ensure that tasks are planned and done.

At the end of the day there may be differences between you that are getting in the way of effective supervision. Asking about approaches, ideas, expectations and so on is better than making assumptions. There may be differences of perception – just because the policy, activity or proposal is obvious to you therefore it must be obvious, the right thing and agreed by your colleague! This leads straight into dealing with clashes between incumbents and curates.

Clashes between you – theology, principles and values

In his book on the Eden project, Tim Smit (2002) draws on Sondheim's musical *Into the Woods* to show that there are at least two views on something. From one completely reasonable perspective (possibly that of a child) the story of Jack and the Beanstalk is a charming tale illustrating courage, resourcefulness and the triumph over adversity. From another perspective it is a story about an amoral little hooligan who climbs a beanstalk, steals things from a big chap who has never done him any harm, and eventually ends up killing him. Yet a third perspective would examine the story from a psychological perspective.

It is inevitable that in a close working relationship there will be differences of perspective, of style, attitudes, beliefs and approaches. Sometimes these differences are serious enough to cause conflict, usually not with the fairytale ending.

There are few certainties in the business of ministry, and many judgements have to be made on the basis of partial information, inadequate knowledge and slender resources. These judgements are very rarely absolute and can give rise to disagreements between incumbent and curate about what should have happened or might happen in any given situation. We looked in Chapter 4 at some of the differences that arise from stances we take and positions we adopt. The question arises of how to deal with them.

The distinctive nature of the curate–incumbent relationship means that there is a mutuality in ministry that derives from both people being shepherds together with a shared responsibility for the flock of Christ. Yet that mutuality is modified by the training context. So far as the incumbent is concerned, overall responsibility for the ministry in the parish lies with him or her. This must be recognized by the incumbent as well as by the curate and, after all the exploration and talking through is completed, direction will be given and authority accepted. So far as the curate is concerned he or she is ministering under the oversight of the incumbent and is to some extent a 'bird of passage'. There will come a time when he or she will be freer to steer things and set the tone of ministry in a future parish, but for the time being direction must be accepted and the incumbent's authority recognized. Freedom is never absolute and mature human beings, incumbents and curates alike, are never free to indulge themselves at the expense of the flock for which Christ died.

In all situations it is part of the loyalty each owes to the other, and part of the professional consistency to be offered to parishioners, that support will be given in public and disagreements addressed in private. The spontaneity with which we react to situations of perceived differences means that personal discipline over when and how much to speak our mind must be developed and exercised with care. This is particularly true where correction or a reprimand from the incumbent is necessary for a curate.

In the end there are few differences that cannot be accommodated within a relationship of mutual trust and respect so long as they are explored openly and honestly with each other and the structures of authority and accountability are recognized and preserved.

Theological reflection – from where do you start?

Much of this book points to the importance of reflecting on experience and learning through a process of reflection. The idea of reflection has recently been taken up into a formal understanding of theology called pastoral theology and now more usually known as practical theology.

Practical theologians believe that it is crucially important to create a bridge between the traditions of the Church as expressed in the Scriptures, doctrine, church history and liturgy on the one hand and our lived experience of life and ministry on the other. The gap between these can appear to be very large. Yet the moment we begin to talk about our experience we already begin to shape it because we use ideas, metaphors and images with which we are familiar. For Christian people some of these concepts will naturally come from within the tradition of faith.

However this conversation between on the one hand experience and on the other church tradition and doctrine creates a fundamental dilemma. Where does one start? Some people want to start from a secure base in truthfulness through Scripture and the revelation of God, being acutely aware that our experience is inevitably flawed and tainted by our involvement in the sin of the world. Others believe that God is in our experience through his ongoing creative activity, and that sometimes our experience will act as an appropriate and proper critique of the Church's way of understanding Scripture and its own life.

To illustrate these approaches we can imagine an incumbent helping a curate with reflection on a sermon preached at a wedding of non-churchgoing people.

One approach is to ask what truth was being communicated to the congregation and the couple themselves. The questions would be designed to elicit how the sermon offered the nature of a Christian marriage, perhaps how such a marriage conforms to ideals of love and faithfulness and fits the purposes of God for bringing about a new heaven and a new earth. Examination could continue by asking how sensitivity to the people who were divorced in the congregation was balanced with, say, reference to the Pauline ideals. The sermon might have assumed that the couple had been living together, but reflection could ask how they were helped in the sermon to continue in their relationship and in their personal walk with God.

The other starting point addresses first the experience, both for the congregation and the couple, of human relationships. The curate might be guided here to reflect on how the sermon made reference to the varied relationships that might be represented in the congregation, of marriage, widowhood, partnership, perhaps civil partnership, and the whole gamut of intimate relationships. The curate might be helped to ask how the sermon acknowledged the memories among members of the congregation of their own significant moments of commitment to another. It might have recognized the fragility of all our intimate relationships, and yet also of their potential for making and remaking us in the image of God the Holy Trinity. Reflection might include raising whether the sermon asked where in our relationships we find examples of the gifts of the Spirit, of love, joy, peace, patience, kindness and so on, and thereby discover and welcome experience of God. Reflection might also ask how the couple had that experience in their relationship already and whether that could be celebrated in the sermon.

Both approaches in supervision in this illustration seek to have the same end, to critique an important moment when the gospel is preached, and support and encouragement is offered to a couple starting their married life. But they start from different positions, and may or may not end up at the same point.

It would be important for a supervisor to recognize where a curate is starting from, and to help him or her to reflect from that point as effectively as possible. It is not the supervisor's job to insist that the curate adopts another starting point. However once effective reflection with the natural method is acquired it could be very useful for an incumbent to offer the other approach, or to suggest trying it together to see what could be learned.

Relations with other ministers

A wise incumbent will be aware that there could be tensions between a curate and other ministers, ordained or lay. In one parish with a well-developed pattern and structure of lay ministries it seemed to the stipendiary curate that there was little for her to do, that she was taken for granted and her own developing pattern of working and her distinctive approach to ministry were not valued. The message being conveyed to her was, 'Ah, you're the new curate. Nice to meet you. Now, what's the next item on the agenda?' In this situation an incumbent will need to create space for the curate to minister and to learn, to make mistakes and to be affirmed, even if this means negotiating a more restricted sphere of activity for others, or asking them to take a back seat for a time.

Jealousy and rivalry can also arise where a new curate is seen by others to threaten their ministry or status in the parish. In an example from another parish opportunity was frequently taken by a long-established reader to put down the curate, criticize her behaviour and disagree with her opinions. It was believed by the curate that her arrival was seen as threatening and she decided after discussion with her incumbent to look for occasions when she could affirm the reader and ask for his advice. This was for the most part an effective strategy and good relations were established. A similar situation could arise where an ordained local minister or part-time NSM, or perhaps a retired priest, feels that their position is under threat from the arrival of a young, lively and popular curate. The incumbent here will want to watch for signs of aggressive language, covert authoritarianism or even bullying as those who feel they are being pushed out seek to bolster their position. One way an incumbent might continue to signal appreciation of the longer-standing ministers would be to delegate a particular part of the curate's training. The incumbent will also want to make sure that his or her time for the others is not diminished in favour of time for the curate. It is not easy to deal with rivalries because these feelings are not usually shared openly, but awareness of problems that might arise, and sensitivity to the emerging signs will be halfway to dealing with them.

In this situation the personal models of ministry being offered to the curate are varied and complex. This richness is a particular bonus for someone newly ordained, but it could be perplexing. This might need exploring in supervision and the incumbent will need to be aware of the confusion that could arise from competing messages, both overt and covert, that the curate is receiving.

An incumbent's sickness, study leave or absence

Most dioceses have clear expectations that an incumbent should not seek to move or be granted study leave until some time in the curate's third year, that is, after the curate has completed at least one year as priest. Nevertheless this policy is occasionally not followed, and whenever a curate finds himself or herself alone in the parish special arrangements must be made.

First the curate will need preparing for the situation. It will be a wonderful learning opportunity – but is likely to be faced with apprehension and uncertainty. In this connection we refer to the discussion about the different types of authority in ministry in Chapter 9. A curate as the sole ordained minister in a parish will often be looked to by laypeople as a source of ministerial authority and guidance. Patterns of dependency are likely to move more in the curate's direction as an incumbent-shaped hole begins to emerge. He or she will need preparing for this, especially in being helped to understand his or her authority and its limits. The curate should be encouraged not to assume the responsibilities and authority of an incumbent.

A curate will need at least three sorts of supervision in the absence or during the long illness of an incumbent. First, there will be the need for a confidential relationship with a wise and experienced priest who can offer guidance and advice and the sort of supervision that the curate has been receiving hitherto. It will usually be the responsibility of the bishop to select and appoint such a person; it may be a retired priest or experienced training incumbent who does not currently have a curate in post.

Second, while the overall ministry will be guided and supported by the churchwardens and PCC, there are some issues of authorizing ministry. Overseeing the priestly ministry in the parish will usually devolve upon the area dean, or occasionally an archdeacon. For instance a question about ministerial practice, such as a marriage of divorced persons, may arise in the parish where there is no policy in place, or guidance might be needed about the suitability of a memorial proposed for the churchyard.

Third, there is also the matter of reporting on the curate's ministry each year. It should be borne in mind that, in the absence of an incumbent, a stipendiary curate is highly likely to look to this person for a reference as he or she eventually seeks to move to another post. Arrangements for this will usually be made by the CME adviser. It could be that an area dean is able to provide all three sorts of supervision; he or she is likely to have more intimate local knowledge of the parish and its situation. The point is that the oversight of the curate in the parish will also have disappeared. It is important that the bishop makes it clear that the wardens and PCC have responsibility for the management of the parish, but not necessarily responsibility for the management of the curate which should reside with the area dean, or some other person appointed by the bishop.

All these decisions will require a careful judgement and a consultation with the curate. In the absence of the incumbent it is unlikely that another colleague from within the parish would be the obvious person to fill the gap. The probable and considerable adjustment of relationship required on both sides is likely to create strain, no matter how skilled the other might be. It would be best for working relationships that already exist to be left alone as those where friendship and casual support and advice can be offered and given, and relationships involving authority to be set up outside the parish.

Not all of these problems will be present in every working relationship, but some may be at times. The next chapter looks particularly at the expectations that are held about curates, where they come from, and at the implications that follow.

Points for reflection

- Who would you look to for advice when difficulties emerge for you and your curate?
- Do you know your curate well enough yet to anticipate what problems might emerge?
- Do you have a supervisor of your own as a training incumbent?
- Is there a chapter of training incumbents with whom to share knowledge and support?
- How often do you tell people rather than show them what to do, and how often do you listen to their ideas about possible solutions?

12

Who shapes the expectations
of curates?

- Where do your expectations of a curacy come from?
- Do you base those expectations on how you were treated as a curate, or on how you think you should have been treated as a curate?
- How important is your own style, background and ideal model of ministry in shaping your expectations of your curate?
- Who is your hero?

How we understand ourselves in ministry is a complex process. Our model of what it means to be a faithful priest and effective leader in the church is derived from many sources. We have already indicated that, for each person, working with their own training incumbent immediately after ordination is a powerful influence on their future ministry. We can react against that model, rejecting what we saw, or we can internalize it and seek to emulate it. For most of us it is a mixture of the two processes that is likely to be influential.

There are other influences of course. What about your own experience? There may have been a priest who guided your vocation and was enormously influential on your early ideas. You could have developed a model of ministry that is influenced by your experience in secular employment – it is not unknown for former managers in industry and commerce to bring into a ministerial career and a church context managerial attitudes and styles that are now part of who they are. Others, perhaps deliberately, avoid working styles and practices of a former profession because they were unfulfilled by them and sought to make a change in their lives.

There are also unconscious influences and memories, that are part of our being, of which we are largely unaware – but they play their powerful part in the background, shaping our ideas of what is appropriate.

Social scientists tell us that a *role* in society is made up of a collection of our and other people's expectations of our behaviour. This is as true of ordained ministerial leadership as it is of checkout operators, solicitors or politicians. The shape of those expectations will be formed by what the Church (as a quasi-employer) expects of its ministers, and by what the preferred church tradition contributes, the theological education, parents, partner and family, the local congregation and its influential members, and so on. We generally take our reference points for what it means to be an ordained leader from a complex network of interacting factors.

The supervisor's expectations

How important for the curate are a supervisor's expectations of him or her? Of course those expectations will in part be formed by diocesan and national church outcomes for the first years after ordination. They will be formed by the curate and what the individual is aware of needing to know, and by what the local church sees as right for their focus of ministry in their particular context. Recent research findings illuminate another source of expectations.

One author's research with curates has been indicated and now a key discovery among those findings is offered. The research method using the model of psychological type is briefly described.

Questionnaire items which conformed to each of the psychological type preferences were created. These were constructed in the language of expectations incumbents might have of curates. Illustrative of a preference for extraversion are 'My training incumbent expected me easily to form friendships with many different people' and 'My training incumbent expected me to enjoy taking the spotlight in ministry'; and of a preference for introversion 'My training incumbent expected me to work well in solitude' and 'My training incumbent expected me to prefer writing to talking.' There were eight other expectations for each of the eight preferences.

Similarly there were items for sensing. For example, 'My training incumbent expected me to pay attention to detail' and '. . . to have a common-sense rather than visionary approach'. For intuition the items included '. . . be imaginative and speculative' and '. . . think in abstract rather than concrete terms'.

There were ten items for thinking, such as 'My training incumbent expected me to be clear about principles' and '. . . not to be influenced by my feelings about people'. For feeling the items included '. . . be gentle rather than tough-minded with people' and '. . . be more aware of people's strengths than their limitations'.

There were ten items for judging, including 'My training incumbent expected me to be organized and systematic' and '. . . to find daily routine a comfortable way to do things'. For perceiving the items included '. . . discover what I wanted to do as I go along' and '. . . pull things together well at the last minute'.

The questionnaire was mailed to 106 curates in five dioceses whose psychological type preferences and those of their incumbents were known. Curates were asked to indicate how far they regarded their incumbents to have each of these 80 expectations of them. Eighty-nine questionnaires were returned and the response data were analysed.

Expectations and psychological type

The analysis showed that there was no relationship between the views the curates held of their incumbents' expectations and their own psychological type profile. Thus the curates' responses did not appear to be influenced by who they were. However a clear relationship was shown to exist between the views the curates held of their incumbents' expectations and the incumbents' psychological type profiles. This was a consistent finding for all the psychological type preferences.

It was concluded that the expectations incumbents held of curates were related to who the incumbents were and not to who the curates were. An example will illustrate the process that appears to be at work. Incumbents with a preference for extraversion expected their curates to behave in a way that is consistent with their own preference for extraversion, for example perhaps to help to get things going socially and to remember names and faces easily. This expectation is independent of whether the curate had a preference for extraversion or introversion. Similarly an incumbent with a preference for thinking held expectations of her or his curate that are representative of that preference – for example perhaps to be wary more than trusting and to be more focused on justice than peace – and this expectation is independent of whether the curate is a thinking or a feeling type.

The importance of this finding is that psychological type is a significant factor in the relationship between incumbents and curates, and that incumbents' expectations of their colleagues are derived from the incumbents, not the curates. This may well be an unconscious or semi-conscious process.

The right expectations

It is clearly important that an incumbent is made aware of any tendency to create expectations of the curate that might be inappropriate. It is also important that incumbents create expectations about a curate's behaviour and attitudes in ministry that are appropriate to the curate they are training.

The research did not examine how far the opposite influence of psychological type was appropriate, that is any expectations that curates had of their supervisors. However working with knowledge of psychological type for both incumbents and curates together will help to eliminate any unconscious or inappropriate bias in the expectations and attitudes that are held by the one of the other.

Are you aware of how your ideal originates? Does it come from your memories of experience of an exceptional priest perhaps, or arise from ideas culled from reading about ministry, or where else?

Some implications from examining the expectations that incumbents hold of their curates have been highlighted here. The final chapter is addressed to the curate.

Points for reflection

- Are you aware of your expectations of your curate?
- Are you more aware of how they originate now?
- Could you invite him or her to tell you where your expectations are felt to be constricting or unhelpful?
- Could you ask your curate to share the expectations he or she has of you?

13

A word to the curate

- Where do your expectations of a curacy come from?
- What do you want out of your first few years of ministry?
- What sort of relationship with a supervisor do you expect?

If you are a newly ordained minister you may well have picked this book up and thought to yourself: 'This is interesting. Is there anything in here I should know?' Perhaps you have purchased it yourself. Although written primarily with incumbents in mind it is recognized that there may be much in the foregoing chapters that curates will find stimulating and helpful.

The questions curates need to ask are about their own relationship with their incumbent. How healthy is it? Are you getting what you need? Do you spend time together? Is the supervision you receive effective? Where are the gaps, where are the problems?

Experience suggests that common tensions arise between colleagues because of different assumptions about minor matters, for example the amount of time to be in church before a service begins, dress at parish events, or what constitutes a sufficient reason to miss a meeting.

If you are unsatisfied, this book may help you to pinpoint exactly what it is you want to change. The first gentle step may be to ask if your incumbent has read this book. He or she may not have seen it and so it could be helpful to give it to him or her. This will enable her or him to review things in a holistic way. It would be better to offer him or her, for a discussion, the same starting base as yourself rather than be tempted to use this book as a resource for your own viewpoint.

Your obvious next step is to talk to your incumbent about your concerns. It may help to remember that you are only one of a number of demands that are made on his or her time, though you may rightly think you are the most important! So in order to be creative rather than complaining it will be useful to identify exactly what it is that you want to change. Be specific. For example, if it is about her or his expectations of you, identify exactly what those expectations are rather than make a general complaint that your incumbent expects too much of you. If it is the case that you feel he or she expects less of you than you could offer, be prepared to make suggestions about the work that she or he could delegate or the responsibility that you might take on. It could be useful to identify these items in relation to your learning goals, or to the type of ministry that you hope to move into after your first post.

In this you will probably want to offer solutions as well as your reasons for dissatisfaction. Be part of the answer, not just the problem.

It may be that you are unhappy about the supervision sessions. Identify exactly what it is you want to change – frequency, venue, agenda balance, preparation, perhaps direction offered more than suggestions. Do you get enough guidance? Where are the gaps – in knowledge, in systems or structures, in the rules and regulations provided by the parish or the diocese?

You may find another look at sections of earlier chapters, 'Getting started', 'Keeping it going', and 'Problems you might encounter', will help you to identify the specifics. When you prepare to initiate a conversation have a look at Appendix 5, 'How to offer criticism' – this may be helpful.

If there is no problem and you feel satisfied then offer your incumbent the feedback that she or he may value. Look at Appendix 4, 'How to give praise' – this also may be helpful. But apart from dissatisfactions and issues that can be sorted out between you in conversation, there are situations where the problems are more serious.

Getting help

All working relationships can be sources of joy, friendship and support. It is good when training incumbents and curates find this to be true in their case. Such relationships are dynamic, and develop and change over time. However, the Church is not immune to human frailty and sin and unfortunately there are cases where a relationship breaks down, trust is eroded and communication stifled. Where a relationship becomes seriously damaged there is a need for honest and courageous reporting at the earliest moment.

Although such a decline in relationship is usually gradual there will be signs early on that something must be done – you start avoiding each other; communication becomes increasingly less face-to-face; you keep disagreeing about the same thing; disagreement about a number of things increases; you challenge each other in public; you, the curate, find yourself making decisions about areas of work without prior consultation, and so on.

It is easy to come with expectations that your training incumbent should be able to handle all things and that if the relationship begins to suffer it will be all his or her fault. One always starts a new area of ministry with high hopes, and these are especially high after such a long time discerning a vocation and looking forward to ordination. Sometimes of course there are flaws and failures that are discovered either in yourself or in your training incumbent, but sometimes it is just the mix that does not work out. Sometimes a relationship breaks down with a training incumbent who has had many happy curates. Sometimes it is just a matter of being chalk and cheese, which neither of you spotted soon enough.

When things go badly wrong

Where there is a need for reporting breakdown in your relationship, the earlier is always the better, even if it feels like disloyalty or making a fuss about something apparently trivial. It is always a mistake to carry on with perhaps the thought: 'Well, I've only got to sit this out' or, 'I shall be thought of as a failure.' The gospel is not advanced by such attitudes and it makes it harder for things to be resolved creatively in the long term. Incumbent-and-curate relationships are always closely observed by church members. It also offers a bad example to others of how to conduct relationships.

Each diocese will be likely to have its own procedures for dealing with serious breakdowns, and reference to diocesan documents may offer guidance. As a general rule a curate might well want to talk over difficulties they are having or report any grievances to one of the CME tutors in the first instance, in order to explore whether the matter can be resolved informally.

Training incumbents may well want to report difficulties to the CME adviser. If things cannot be sorted out at this level the CME adviser will want to report the situation to an archdeacon or bishop.

At some stage formal procedures for resolving grievances will be appropriate and these are likely to involve written submissions and interviews. These will be specific to each diocese and to the national Church and need no further comment here.

Where very exceptional circumstances require the termination of a curacy before the agreed time, a second curacy is usually found where the training can continue. This is always a solution of last resort since it necessarily involves damage limitation and it probably leaves behind personal problems for incumbent and curate, and disappointments in the parish. These can be very hard to resolve.

Jesus was very clear in his teaching that those who are reconciled to God should seek reconciliation with those who have offended against them or those for whom they have been a cause of offence. Reconciliation involves understanding what has happened and how it has affected the other party. Acknowledging the depth of hurt and anger is a key part of restoring the relationship, even if it cannot return to a previous satisfactory level and those involved agree to move on perhaps more apart than before.

It has been an aim of this book to increase the understanding of the complexities of supervisory relationships and to facilitate reasonable expectations and ways of working such that situations of irretrievable breakdown occur even more rarely than they might do otherwise.

All that may seem rather heavy and you may also have spotted something in this book about how you learn, and about how you want to focus your learning in these early years of public ministry. One of the fundamental things those in ordained ministry have discovered is that the first three years are crucial for setting disciplines of prayer, ministry and learning that they will be renewing throughout many years of healthy and fulfilling ministry.

Questions to the curate

- Are you satisfied with the progress of your training?
- Do you have a comfortable relationship with your supervisor?
- Can you say so if you have – and be specific about what you appreciate?
- Do you know how to raise concerns if you are not satisfied?
- If not, do you know who to talk to about it, other than other curates?

Appendix 1
Biblical images of supervision

BY ALAN WILSON, BISHOP OF BUCKINGHAM

Ecclesiology

Ministerial supervision is not a discrete activity, like mowing the lawn or peeling potatoes. Starting from Gabriel Hebert's illuminating observation that 'the Church exists that Christ may reign',[1] oversight is a human expression of Christ's authority as head, through the medium of relationships held within his structured body.

In Scripture, God acts to save the world through an ordered community. Israel is supervised according to a God-given, evolving order – judges, kings, priests in the old covenant and apostles, elders and 'overseers' in the new. The theocratic vision centred on David survived the exilic destruction of the monarchy and priesthood. Indeed longing for Davidic rule was only strengthened and refocused by exile. The Church of the New Testament emerges from the aspiration that the time is coming in which God 'will restore the kingdom to Israel'.[2] If Christians are 'the refounded Israel of God through being partakers in the Messiah's death',[3] the ordering of the new covenant must reflect and extend the structure of the old. The Christian Church is therefore, of essence, a supervised community.

One of the earliest New Testament communities is described as a flock, over which God has appointed elders as overseers.[4] The Epistle to the Philippians indicates a developing ministry of oversight within early Christianity.[5] St Luke uses the terminology of three-fold ministry, for the officials if not the formal offices of the primitive Church.[6] By the time of the Pastoral Epistles the classic three-fold pattern of bishops, priests and deacons was emerging.[7] This grew from the earlier two-fold pattern, of presbyter–overseers, and deacons.[8] Clement's first letter to the Corinthians illustrates how early ecclesiology was influenced by concepts drawn from the world of civic oversight. By the second century the principal functions of presbyters appear to have been service or leadership (*leitourgia*) and oversight (*episkope*).[9]

A more settled episcopal order was emerging, however. Soon after we find Ignatius of Antioch claiming a more than local episcopal authority among the communities through which he passed on his way to martyrdom in Rome. 'We should look upon the bishop even as we would look upon the Lord himself.'[10]

> See that you all follow the bishop even as Jesus Christ does the Father, and the presbytery as you would the apostles; and reverence the deacons as being the institution of God. Let no man do anything connected with the Church without the bishop.[11]

From here in the Latin West, episcopal supervision became ever more important an element of ecclesiology. It became the lynchpin of Cyprian's vision of the Church, its unity secured by a single episcopate.[12] Thus were laid the foundations for later monarchical episcopacy – what the Puritans were one day to call 'prelacy'. The theological and historical questions this raises are far outside the scope of this account, but we may ask in this context how was the ministry of 'oversight' exercised within the Christian community? What kind of ministry has it been and can it be?

The practice of *episkope*

Two practical elements are inherent in *episkope*: presence (being there) and seeing what is going on (compare the Hebrew Qal[13]). We do not have to engage in high-level language games to establish a basic correspondence between *episkope* and the Latin *supervisio*. Four functions define the 'oversight' of God's people, as they grow from their scriptural roots into the structured community of the Church – shepherding, teaching, stewardship and priesthood.

Shepherds

However greatly any suggestion that they are 'sheep' may jar against modern Christian susceptibilities, the language of shepherding is much used of God's people in Old and New Testaments, and remains fundamental to Christian leadership.[14] Refined by the parallel concept of Davidic kingship, this central pillar of Christian ecclesiology has deep roots in the ministry of Christ himself. In St Mark's Gospel, the crowds who see Jesus take the road to Jerusalem hail him as one who comes in the name of the Lord, to restore the kingdom of their father David.[15] In his discourse in the temple courts, Jesus carefully establishes his relationship to David. What does David himself mean, by describing the Messiah as his 'Lord' if he is only his Son, in a subsidiary way?[16] Thus Jesus is given to (and received by) the community of faith as what Montgomery's hymn calls 'Great David's greater Son'. This imagery is reported as a central element in the preaching of the first Christian community.[17]

The practice of Davidic kingship is closely associated with shepherding:

> [The Lord] chose his servant David
> and took him from the sheepfolds:
> from tending the nursing ewes he brought him
> to be the shepherd of his people Jacob,
> of Israel, his inheritance.
> With upright heart he tended them;
> and guided them with skilful hand.[18]

This vision of leadership under God has deep resonances in Hebrew tradition. The judges are seen as those whom God provided to shepherd his people Israel.[19] Moses selected Joshua to be his deputy, so that 'the congregation of the Lord may not be like sheep without a shepherd'.[20] We find the same striking picture of God's people scattered used by the prophet Micaiah Ben Imlah[21] and on the lips of Jesus in Matthew's and Mark's Gospels.[22] God himself is, ultimately, the 'Shepherd of Israel', who 'lead[s] Joseph like a flock'.[23]

The prime task of the shepherd is to keep the flock together, to provide for its nurture and safety.[24] Against this background, the Jesus of St John's Gospel declares: 'I am the Good Shepherd.'[25] In this passage, Jesus contrasts himself to the hireling whose sheep fall prey to wolves. Because they are not his own, the hireling will not pay the cost of his life to protect them. Early Christian tradition calls Jesus 'the great shepherd of the sheep'.[26] In the first letter of Peter, the term 'shepherd' parallels 'overseer' (bishop) and refers to God himself.[27] The same writer offers his faithful fellow presbyter–overseers the prospect of an unfading crown of glory when 'the Chief Shepherd appears'.[28] Shepherding extends from this world to the world to come in the Apocalypse, which pictures Christ at the end of time, as in the twenty-third psalm, leading his flock to 'springs of living water'.[29]

Teachers

Beginning with Moses, *Moshe Rabbenu*, a central ministry among the people of God has been teaching. An 'ordination' modelled on the tradition that Moses laid hands on Joshua[30] conferred teaching authority on the *Ribbi* within Jewish communities from biblical times to the fourth century CE.[31] An important duty of Levitical priests in the Second Temple was to teach the people the law.[32] This responsibility was not academic, but extended to every aspect of ordinary life. The Levites' teaching authority derived from their position as the guardians and exponents of Torah – Israel's glory.

The Wisdom tradition in the Old Testament sees the giving and receiving of instruction as a blessing. Fathers of households have a special responsibility to teach, and children to learn from them.[33] Within families and communities, openness to instruction is seen as a key to material and spiritual prosperity:

> Keep hold of instruction; do not let go;
> guard her, for she is your life.[34]

Behind all earthly teaching activity stands God himself. 'See, God is exalted in his power. Who is a teacher like him?[35] The prophet Jeremiah compares idols unfavourably with the God of Israel, because they cannot teach – 'the instruction given by idols is no better than wood!'[36] God is pictured as the teacher of his people, frustrated at their unwillingness to accept his teaching.[37] As well as fathers in families and God himself, the Old Testament lays a special teaching responsibility upon priests:

> The lips of a priest should guard knowledge, and people should seek instruction from his mouth, for he is the messenger of the LORD of hosts. But you have turned aside from the way; you have caused many to stumble by your instruction; you have corrupted the covenant of Levi, says the LORD of hosts, and so I make you despised and abased before all the people, inasmuch as you have not kept my ways, but have shown partiality in your instruction.[38]

Once the temple and its priesthood had been destroyed, the core of Jewish religion became the teaching of the great rabbis.[39]

Within the emerging Christian community also, teaching played a great part. In Matthew's Gospel Jesus instructs his disciples: 'not to be called Rabbi for you have one teacher and you are all students'.[40] However, the title seems to have been used freely for Jesus in the Gospels by friend and foe alike.[41] In John's Gospel, Nicodemus confesses by faith that Jesus is 'a teacher who has come from God'.[42]

A core element in the first Jerusalem community, alongside its fellowship, the breaking of bread and prayer, was the apostles' teaching.[43] It is plain throughout the Acts of the Apostles that this instruction, like Levitical teaching, was more than academic, encompassing every aspect of the Christian Way.[44]

A large part of St Paul's ministry within his disciple communities was that of the trained rabbi he was, 'warning everyone and teaching everyone in all wisdom'.[45] His responsibility was to teach all aspects of discipleship, after the wisdom pattern, positioning himself in a fatherly relationship to members of his churches.[46] Teaching was not an apostolic monopoly – it figures in the general list of gifts of the Holy Spirit in Ephesians 4.[47] All the same, teaching is an important task for the presbyter–bishop in the Pastoral Epistles. As the locus of oversight, he must 'have a firm grasp of the word that is trustworthy in accordance with the teaching, so that he may be able both to preach sound doctrine and to refute those who contradict it'.[48]

Therefore a candidate for this order should be 'an apt teacher'.[49] A similar responsibility is laid in these letters on Timothy,[50] and all God's servants.[51] Conversely, the apostolic literature abounds in warnings against false teachers.[52]

The giving and receiving of instruction is a central responsibility of those who oversee the people of God in Old and New Testaments. In the apostolic age this responsibility came increasingly, but not exclusively, to rest on teaching presbyter–bishops, or 'overseers'. Thus the apostolic deposit of faith was protected, while supporting the exercise of spiritual gifts and sound discipleship. Authoritative teaching was the natural extension, after Jesus' ascension, of his ministry, who St Matthew says taught 'as one having authority, and not as their scribes'.[53]

Stewards

One biblical sign of authority from God is the ability to make things happen – what Isaiah calls (applying Davidic imagery to Eliakim) 'the key of the house of David – he shall open and no one shall shut; he shall shut and no one shall open'.[54]

In St Matthew's Gospel Jesus speaks of Peter in parallel terms, holding the keys of the Kingdom.[55] In St John's upper room, a similar power to remit and retain sins is breathed over the first apostles.[56] This authority is not, however, absolute. It is delegated and exercised as stewardship.

The story of Joseph paints a classic picture of an ancient Near Eastern household, run from day to day by a 'steward'.[57] This profession figures largely in Jesus' parables of the Kingdom which picture his disciples as stewards, expected to conduct themselves responsibly in the absence of their master.[58]

> Who then is the faithful and wise slave, whom the master has put in charge of his household, to give the other slaves their allowance of food at the proper time? Blessed is that slave whom his master will find at work when he arrives. Truly I tell you, he will put that one in charge of all his possessions. But if that wicked slave says to himself, 'My master is delayed,' and he begins to beat his fellow slaves and eats and drinks with drunkards, the master of that slave will come on a day when he does not expect him and at an hour that he does not know. He will cut him in pieces and put him with the hypocrites, where there will be weeping and gnashing of teeth.[59]

In this parable some disciples are set over others, responsible for the daily management of the master's estate. They are to arrange for the due feeding of the other servants under them. The original context may be scribes set over God's household.[60] In Luke the parable is the answer to Peter's question about the watchful servant, 'Lord, are you telling this parable for us, or for everyone?'[61] Luke's implicit answer is that, members as they were of a community within which 'you are all brothers', apostles carry with their position in the Christian community a special degree of stewardship. Interestingly, Luke makes the subject of these words *oikonomos* – a 'steward' or 'bailiff' rather than just, as in Matthew, *doulos*, 'servant' in the general sense.

Elsewhere in the New Testament, apostolic ministry is described as the ordering or stewardship of a household.[62] Paul describes this 'anxiety for all the churches' as his greatest burden:[63] 'Think of us in this way, as servants of Christ and stewards of God's mysteries.'[64]

In the Pastoral Epistles, where the ministry of oversight is more clearly described than anywhere else in the New Testament, the presbyter–bishop is described as the *oikonomos* of God.[65] This picture exerts a central and abiding influence on Christian leadership. The abbot in the Rule of Benedict, for example, is to be above all 'a worthy steward over God's House'.[66]

Although stewardship of the highest order is particularly required of those in church leadership, all disciples are stewards in some sense of the term. Thus, in the first letter of Peter, Christians are called to be 'good stewards of the manifold grace of God'.[67] They are to do this by acts of love and service inspired and empowered by God's grace, with two specific examples given – 'speaking the very words of God' and service 'with the strength that God supplies'. 'Servanthood', then, is not a weak concept. It does not indicate someone who habitually rolls over and says 'yes'. Rather it belongs to those who bear the delegated power to manage of the *oikonomos* – substantial, authoritative stewardship exercised on behalf of the master.

Mediators

In Old and New Testament God nearly always works through people. On one occasion in the book of Exodus we hear of the 70 elders going up the mountain and eating with God, seeing him directly.[68] The rest of the time God is experienced through the mediation of others, angels and people, whose task is to act and speak for him. Within the Pentateuchal community, the Levites actualize and mediate God's relationship to his people, sacralizing everyday life by interfacing priests and people.[69] Part of this calling is to act, on occasion, as the instruments of God's wrath.[70] God makes Moses a greater mediator than the priests or his Levite ancestors[71] by appointing him as his personal ambassador; then, in the face of his spokesman's protestations, Aaron the Levite as his assistant:

You shall speak to him and put the words in his mouth; and I will be with your mouth and with his mouth and teach you what you shall do. He indeed shall speak for you to the people; he shall serve as a mouth for you, and you shall serve as God for him.[72]

Mediatory responsibilities are also assigned in the Old Testament to David,[73] the prophets[74] and teachers of wisdom,[75] Balaam and even, by implication, Balaam's Ass.[76] The whole people take on a mediatory function in St Paul's view of Israel as the nation 'entrusted with the oracles of God'.[77]

Like Moses before him, Jesus is God's spokesman, a 'teacher sent from God'. A defining moment in the establishment of Jesus' authority among his apostles is the transfiguration, with Jesus shining in glory alongside the prophetic mediators of the faith of Israel, Moses and Elijah.[78] The apostles and especially Peter appear in the Acts as God's spokesmen, mediating knowledge of his will to the people, and acting in his name.[79] In the letter to the Hebrews, the priestly function of mediation is focused on Jesus. The Son of God is a priest who embodies and transcends the sole priesthood of Melchizedek.[80] The effect of Jesus' mediatory priesthood is not to abolish priesthood, but rather to establish a 'new covenant',[81] in which priesthood is distributed among all God's people. The first letter of Peter calls the whole community of the Church, a 'holy priesthood, to offer spiritual sacrifices acceptable to God through Jesus Christ'.[82] This calling articulates God's light and will within the world.[83] The mediatory calling prefigured in Moses and supremely embodied in Jesus is thus spread among all Christians. In 1 Peter this mediatorial role applies not only to relationships with the outer world, but also to the way in which God's varied grace is ministered within the gathered community of the Church. This parallels St Paul's vision of Christian ministry as a 'ministry of reconciliation'.[84]

This function of mediation arises from God's life among his people. It is not so clearly focused on 'overseers' as the ministries of shepherds, teachers and stewards. Those with supervisory responsibility, however, have a special responsibility to establish and sustain relationships in God's name. In the Greek East, episcopacy has never been seen in the kind of juridical terms that have defined it in the Latin West. Orthodox theology describes it mainly by its priestliness, as a necessary locus of the image of Christ in the eucharistic mystery – a mediatorial identity in relation to the community of faith.[85]

(Quotations from the Bible in Appendix 1 are taken from the New Revised Standard Version, Anglicized edition, 1989, 1995.)

Notes to Appendix 1

1 Hebert, A. G. (1944), *The Form of the Church*, London, Faber, p. 123.
2 Acts 1.9.
3 Ramsey, M. (1956), *The Gospel and the Catholic Church*, London, Longmans Green, p. 6.
4 Acts 20.28.
5 Lightfoot, J. B. (1873), *St Paul's Epistle to the Philippians*, London, pp. 179, 267.
6 Acts 20.28; 14.23; 6.1–6.
7 Shown, e.g., in 1 Timothy 3.2 (bishops); 5.7 (presbyters); 3.8, 12 (deacons).
8 Von Campenhausen, H. (1969), *Ecclesiastical Authority and Spiritual Power in the Church of the First Three Centuries*, Peabody, Mass., Hendrickson, pp. 84–8.
9 *Ad Corinth.* 44 1–3, quoted in Schillebeeckx, E. (1985), *The Church with a Human Face*, London, SCM, p. 125.
10 Ignatius to the Ephesians cap. 6, Ante Nicene Fathers Christian Library.
11 Ignatius to the Smyrnaeans cap. 8, Ante Nicene Fathers Christian Library.
12 Cyprian Epistle 55. 24, quoted in Bévenot, M. (1957), *Cyprian: The Lapsed and the Unity of the Catholic Church*, London, Newman, pp. 108–9.
13 Brown, F., Driver, S. and Briggs, C. (1996), *The Brown-Driver-Briggs Hebrew and English Lexicon*, Peabody, Mass., Hendrickson, pp. 823–4 [*Qal*] 'observe' (*Aia*) 'visit' (A2) 'review' (A4) and [*hiph'îl*] 'appoint' (B).
14 Nelson, J. (ed.) (1966), *Management and Ministry*, Norwich, MODEM, pp. 7–8.
15 Mark 11.9–10.
16 Mark 12.35–7.
17 Acts 2.34–5.
18 Psalm 78.70–2. Cp. 1 Chronicles 11.2 // 2 Samuel 5.2.
19 2 Samuel 7.7 // 1 Chronicles 17.6.
20 Numbers 27.17.
21 1 Kings 22.17 // 2 Chronicles 18.16.
22 Matthew 9.16 // Mark 6.34. Cp. Mark 14.27 (Zechariah 13.7), Zechariah 10.2.
23 Psalm 80.1. Cp. Ezekiel 34.15.
24 Ezekiel 34.
25 John 10.11, 14.
26 Hebrews 13.20.
27 1 Peter 2.25.
28 1 Peter 5.4.
29 Revelation 7.17.
30 Numbers 27.22–3.
31 Jacobs, L. (1995), *The Jewish Religion – A Companion*, Oxford, Oxford University Press, p. 401.
32 Nehemiah 8.7–8.
33 For example Proverbs 4.1; 13.1; 15.5.
34 Proverbs 4.13.

35 Job 36.22.
36 Jeremiah 10.8.
37 Jeremiah 17.23; 32.33; 35.13.
38 Malachi 2.6–9.
39 Sanders, E. P. (1992), *Judaism – Practice and Belief 63 BCE–66 CE*, London, SCM Press and Philadelphia, Trinity Press International, p. 416.
40 Matthew 23.8.
41 By Judas (Matthew 26.25; Mark 14.45), Peter (Mark 9.5; 11.21), blind Bartimaeus (Mark 10.51).
42 John 3.2.
43 Acts 2.42.
44 For example, discipline (Acts 5.1–11 – Ananias and Sapphira), the structuring of the community (Acts 6.1–6 – Stephen and the seven deacons), strategic planning (Acts 13.1–3 – the mission of Barnabas and Saul).
45 Colossians 1.28.
46 1 Corinthians 4.14–15.
47 Ephesians 4.11.
48 Titus 1.9.
49 1 Timothy 3.2.
50 1 Timothy 4.11.
51 2 Timothy 2.2.
52 Like 2 Corinthians 11.13; 1 Timothy 1.3–7; Jude 4; Hebrews 13.9; 1 John 4.4–6; 2 Peter 2.1–3; Revelation 2.14, 20.
53 Matthew 7.28–9.
54 Isaiah 22.22.
55 Matthew 16.18–19.
56 John 20.23.
57 Genesis 43.16, 19; 44.1, 4.
58 See, for example, Mark 12.1–11 (// Matthew 21.33–44; Luke 20.9–18 – the wicked tenants); Matthew 18.23–35 (unforgiving servants); Matthew 20.1–16 (workers in the vineyard); Matthew 25.14–30 (// Luke 19.12–27 – the talents); Luke 16.1–8 (dishonest steward); Luke 17.7–10 (the servant's reward).
59 Matthew 24.45–51 // Luke 12.42–6.
60 Fenton, J. (1963), *Saint Matthew*, London, Pelican, p. 394.
61 Luke 12.41.
62 In 1 Timothy 3.15, the Church is described as God's 'household'.
63 2 Corinthians 11.28.
64 1 Corinthians 4.1.
65 Titus 1.7.
66 Cary-Elwes, C. and Wybourne, C. (1992), *Work and Prayer – The Rule of Benedict for Lay People*, Tunbridge Wells, Burns & Oates, p. 158.
67 1 Peter 4.10.
68 Exodus 24.9–11.
69 Jacobs, *The Jewish Religion*, p. 135.
70 Exodus 32.25–9.

71 Exodus 2.1.
72 Exodus 4.8–16.
73 1 Chronicles 16.2; 17.16–22. Cp. Psalm 132.10.
74 Both former (Samuel – 1 Samuel 3) and latter prophets (Jeremiah 19.2–13). 'Surely the LORD God does nothing, without revealing his secret to his servants the prophets' (Amos 3.7).
75 'My tongue is like the pen of a ready scribe' (verses addressed 'to the King' – Psalm 45.1).
76 Numbers 23.5, 16; 22.21–33.
77 Romans 3.2.
78 Matthew 17.1–5. Cp. 2 Peter 1.16–18.
79 See e.g. the prayer of Peter and John in Acts 4.24–31.
80 Hebrews 3.1–6; 5.5–7.
81 Hebrews 8.1–2.
82 1 Peter 2.5.
83 1 Peter 2.9–10.
84 1 Peter 4.7–11; 2 Corinthians 5.18–20.
85 Meyendorff, J. (1983), *Byzantine Theology – Historical Trends and Doctrinal Themes*, New York, Fordham, pp. 209–10.

Appendix 2
The Francis Psychological Type Scales

The following list contains pairs of characteristics. For each pair place *one* tick next to that characteristic which is *closer* to the real you, even if you feel both characteristics apply to you. Tick the one that better reflects the real you, even if other people see you differently.

PLEASE COMPLETE EVERY QUESTION

Do you tend to be more...
    active   or   reflective

Do you tend to be more...
    interested in facts   or   interested in theories

Do you tend to be more...
    concerned for harmony   or   concerned for justice

Do you tend to be more...
    happy with routine   or   unhappy with routine

Are you more...
    private   or   sociable

Are you more...
    inspirational   or   practical

Are you more...
    analytic   or   sympathetic

Are you more...
    structured   or   open-ended

Do you prefer...
    having many friends   or   a few deep friendships

Do you prefer...
    the concrete   or   the abstract

Do you prefer...
    feeling   or   thinking

Do you prefer...
    to act on impulse   or   to act on decisions

Do you...
    dislike parties   or   like parties

Do you...
    prefer to design   or   prefer to make

Do you...
    tend to be firm   or   tend to be gentle

Do you . . .
   like to be in control   or   like to be adaptable

Are you . . .
   energized by others   or   drained by too many people

Are you . . .
   conventional   or   inventive

Are you . . .
   critical   or   affirming

Are you . . .
   happier working alone   or   happier working in groups

Do you tend to be more . . .
   socially detached   or   socially involved

Do you tend to be more . . .
   concerned for meaning   or   concerned for detail

Do you tend to be more . . .
   logical   or   humane

Do you tend to be more . . .
   orderly   or   easygoing

Are you more . . .
   talkative   or   reserved

Are you more . . .
   sensible   or   imaginative

Are you more . . .
   tactful   or   truthful

Are you more . . .
   spontaneous   or   organized

Are you mostly . . .
   an introvert   or   an extravert

Are you mostly focused on . . .
   present realities   or   future possibilities

Are you mostly . . .
   trusting   or   sceptical

Are you mostly . . .
   leisurely   or   punctual

Do you . . .
   speak before thinking   or   think before speaking

Do you prefer to . . .
   improve things   or   keep things as they are

Do you . . .
   seek for truth   or   seek for peace

Do you . . .
   dislike detailed planning   or   like detailed planning

Are you . . .
   happier with uncertainty   or   happier with certainty

Are you . . .
    up in the air   or   down to earth
Are you . . .
    warm-hearted   or   fair-minded
Are you . . .
    systematic   or   casual

Now turn over for the scoring key. . . .

Orientation: introversion and extraversion

Find the pairs of items in the box below in the scales overleaf. One tick scores one point, where the item is blank enter 0. These are the items designed to differentiate between extraversion (E) and introversion (I). Now add up the two columns. The higher score indicates your psychological preference and the difference between them indicates the clarity of your preference between them. If both columns add up to five, count yourself as preferring introversion.

- Does your self-assessment from Chapter 5 and the FPTS agree or disagree?
- What did you learn about yourself from this?

extraversion			introversion	
active		or	reflective	
sociable		or	private	
having many friends		or	a few deep friendships	
likes parties		or	dislikes parties	
energized by others		or	drained by too many people	
happier working in groups		or	happier working alone	
socially involved		or	socially detached	
talkative		or	reserved	
an extravert		or	an introvert	
speak before thinking		or	think before speaking	
Total E score			**Total I score**	

Perceiving process: gathering information

Find the pairs of items in the box below in the scales overleaf. One tick scores one point, where the item is blank enter 0. These are the items designed to differentiate between sensing (S) and intuition (N). Now add up the two columns. The higher score indicates your psychological preference and the difference between them indicates the clarity of your preference between them. If both columns add up to five, count yourself as preferring intuition.

- Does your self-assessment from Chapter 5 and the FPTS agree or disagree?
- What did you learn about yourself from this?

sensing		or	intuition	
interested in facts		or	interested in theories	
practical		or	inspirational	
the concrete		or	the abstract	
prefer to make		or	prefer to design	
conventional		or	inventive	
concerned about detail		or	concerned for meaning	
sensible		or	imaginative	
present realities		or	future possibilities	
keep things as they are		or	improve things	
down to earth		or	up in the air	
Total S score			**Total N score**	

Judging process: making decisions

Find the pairs of items in the box below in the scales overleaf. One tick scores one point, where the item is blank enter 0. These are the items designed to differentiate between thinking (T) and feeling (F). Now add up the two columns. The higher score indicates your psychological preference and the difference between them indicates the clarity of your preference between them. If both columns add up to five, count yourself as preferring feeling.

- Does your self-assessment from Chapter 5 and the FPTS agree or disagree?
- What did you learn about yourself from this?

thinking		or	feeling	
concern for justice		or	concern for harmony	
analytic		or	sympathetic	
thinking		or	feeling	
tend to be firm		or	tend to be gentle	
critical		or	affirming	
logical		or	humane	
truthful		or	tactful	
sceptical		or	trusting	
seek for truth		or	seek for peace	
fair-minded		or	warm-hearted	
Total T score			**Total F score**	

Attitude towards the outer world: a 'lifestyle' preference

Find the pairs of items in the box below in the scales overleaf. One tick scores one point, where the item is blank enter 0. These are the items designed to differentiate between judging (J) and perceiving (P). Now add up the two columns. The higher score indicates your psychological preference and the difference between them indicates the clarity of your preference between them. If both columns add up to five, count yourself as preferring perceiving.

- Does your self-assessment from Chapter 5 and the FPTS agree or disagree?
- What did you learn about yourself from this?

judging			perceiving	
happy with routine		or	unhappy with routine	
structured		or	open-ended	
act on decisions		or	act on impulse	
like to be in control		or	like to be adaptable	
orderly		or	easygoing	
organized		or	spontaneous	
punctual		or	leisurely	
like detailed planning		or	dislike detailed planning	
happier with certainty		or	happier with uncertainty	
systematic		or	casual	
Total J score			**Total P score**	

Combining the letters for each of the lists for the highest score will give you some idea of your psychological type, for example, IFNP, ESTJ. The letters combine into 16 different psychological types and a further exploration about type can best be undertaken by attending a Myers–Briggs basic workshop.

The Francis Psychological Type Scales, although verified and reliable, are still a fairly recent contribution to the study of typology. Professor Francis is keen to collect FPTS data from clergy in order to advance his study with the model of psychological type among clergy.

If you would like to help with Professor Francis's research, please send a photocopy of the way in which you have responded to the 40 pairs of items in the questionnaire to:

The Revd Professor Leslie Francis
Welsh National Centre for Religious Education,
University of Wales, Bangor
Meirion, Normal Site
Bangor, LL57 2PZ.

He would be most grateful if you would also kindly include the following personal details: age, gender, type of ministry (e.g. stipendiary, NSM), year of ordination, national Church (e.g. Church of England, Methodist, Church in Wales).

The information will be stored in a computer entirely for statistical purposes. If you include your name and address this will not be included in the data file.

Appendix 3
Psychological type tables of supervising incumbents and curates

MBTI type data for curates and incumbents

All curates

N =   175

ISTJ	ISFJ	INFJ	INTJ
8	22	20	16
4.57%	12.57%	11.43%	9.14%

ISTP	ISFP	INFP	INTP
0	3	17	7
0.00%	1.71%	9.71%	4.00%

ESTP	ESFP	ENFP	ENTP
0	4	16	6
0.00%	2.29%	9.14%	3.43%

ESTJ	ESFJ	ENFJ	ENTJ
12	10	25	9
6.86%	5.71%	14.29%	5.14%

All training incumbents

N =   175

ISTJ	ISFJ	INFJ	INTJ
16	19	13	16
9.14%	10.86%	7.43%	9.14%

ISTP	ISFP	INFP	INTP
2	3	13	7
1.14%	1.71%	8.57%	4.00%

ESTP	ESFP	ENFP	ENTP
1	2	21	6
0.57%	1.14%	11.43%	3.43%

ESTJ	ESFJ	ENFJ	ENTJ
11	10	23	12
6.29%	5.71%	12.57%	6.86%

© David R. Tilley (2005)

Appendix 4
How to give praise

It doesn't come easy to most people in a Western protestant culture to give praise. We have absorbed too many messages that give us low self-worth. Few of us receive enough praise. Positive strokes, praise, recognition, attention and appreciation all raise our sense of fulfilment, achievement and increase our confidence.

Nine rules for giving praise

1 Praise must be genuine. Make sure you really feel the person deserves praise. If it is not genuine your body language will expose you and it will be perceived as flattery or manipulation.
2 Praise is best given spontaneously, naturally and honestly and from the heart. Because this praise is unpredictable it is often seen as more genuine and sincere than praise that might be expected.
3 Praise should be specific. 'Your presentation to the PCC was clear and succinct. It helped them understand the issues' is much better than 'You made a good presentation to the PCC'.
4 Praise doesn't have to include superlatives or extravagant language. Sometimes an unexpected 'thank you' at the right time, with a small gift, can say a great deal more than many words.
5 Make eye contact, show that you have been listening, and pay complete attention.
6 Praise is best given as soon as possible; then it will have most effect. If people are not present, write or call them.
7 Pass it on. 'I was just over at the parish office and Brenda was saying she was extremely satisfied with the software you sorted out for them. You did a good job.'
8 Show you are trying to learn something from the other person. 'The organist was very impressed with the sensitive prayers you used at the funeral. Would you tell me where you got them from?'
9 Celebrate achievement. When something has gone really well buy your curate lunch or an evening meal – why not involve partners as well?

Appendix 5
How to offer criticism

Criticism creates opportunity for the colleague to learn and become more effective. The problem is that colleagues often become defensive and their energy goes into defending rather than learning. If criticism is offered constructively the balance can be tipped. Be sure you have the best interests of your colleague and his or her ministry at heart and then go for it!

Eight rules for offering criticism

1 Always criticize the behaviour or action, not the person.
2 Avoid generalizations. Be specific. It is the detailed example that enables people to learn.
3 Ask 'How do you think you could improve things?' Avoid doing all the talking.
4 Give positive suggestions about how things could improve. This will make it constructive.
5 Criticize in an honest and straightforward way. Avoid half-truths.
6 Always criticize in private.
7 Check back at a later date that what you think you said has been heard correctly. In an emotional moment the memory can get distorted.
8 Avoid mixing criticism with praise. Keep focused. Your colleague will suspect a hidden agenda when you next praise and will not value it.

Appendix 6
Pastoral visiting record form

This is adapted from Appendix B in Foskett and Lyall (1988).

Date of visit:

Number of visit:

Initials of parishioner/patient:

Location of interview:

Length of interview:

Known facts

Include all the known details about the person being visited – age, sex, religious affiliation, reason for visit, etc. – the situation and the occasion of the visit.

Supervisor's comments

Background, observations and assumptions

Include plans and expectations for the visit, what you observed and felt as it began, the appearance of the person visited, etc.

Summary of visit

Record an overview of the visit including your thoughts and feelings, observations and intuitions.

Analysis	Supervisor's comments

Analysis

Person

Record here what you think the person was feeling and thinking during the interview and how he or she is as a result of it.

Visitor

Record what was happening to you during the interview, where you think you succeeded and/or failed in your offering of pastoral care.

Theological reflection

Record here the implicit and explicit beliefs and meanings expressed. Note any themes or associations with biblical or theological ideas. Discuss any ethical issues or dilemmas.

Future aims

Record what you hope or intend to do next.

Why this conversation?

Record here why you chose to write up this conversation and what you feel and think about it now.

Appendix 7
Example of supervision preparation sheet

For the supervision discussion

Date:

I need help or a decision from you about the following:

I'm having a problem with the following:

I'm planning to:

I've made progress in the following areas:

Happiness:

If 1 is 'suicidal' and 10 'The happiest I've ever been' the number I would put down now is

Please pray for me about the following:

Appendix 8
Sample learning contract

From the Diocese of Oxford continuing ministerial education learning contract (Year 200_)

Name:

Parish:

Telephone:

E-mail:

I wish to study the following areas this year for my own development:
(Choose one method below)

- Portfolio
  I might be interested in registering for a Brookes award: Yes/No

- Other recognized academic award
  If you are intending to enrol or continue on a course, please complete the following:

  Title of course:

  Academic institution:

  Duration of course:

  What work are you expected to cover in this academic year?

  Course supervisor/tutor:

- Other learning track (to be negotiated)

Signed: Date:

Signed by incumbent:

Appendix 9

Recommendations for the education of training incumbents in supervision skills

A successful supervising incumbent will be able to:

- Model lifelong learning and effective, reflective ministry which is mission-shaped
- Give an account of a variety of pedagogical methods for skills-based learning and apply them to the context of curacy, suggesting incremental activities to meet the range of published learning outcomes
- Identify and build relationships with others who share responsibility for the curate's learning, including laypeople within the Church, ecumenical and secular partners
- Give a theological and experiential account of the importance of supervision in the life of the Church
- Give a theological and experiential critique of a variety of models of oversight, accountability and supervision from within and beyond the Christian tradition
- Structure an appropriate supervision relationship, e.g. through a learning covenant, with a training incumbent
- Help the training minister to handle the supervision/oversight relationship (establish boundaries) within multi-layered community of relationships (the local ministry setting and other shared tasks)
- Work within the competence level of the training minister
- Support and challenge the training minister
- Work with the obvious issues of ministry and development and the hidden dynamics of projection and power relationships
- Make effective use of the supervision for their supervisory role
- Write evidence-based reports and discuss these with their training minister.

It is envisaged that training in supervision skills, in particular, might be delivered by an academic institution belonging to the local regional partnership. Several such courses are now running at M level, for example, through Anglia Polytechnic University, delivered by the Cambridge Theological Federation. The syllabus covers such topics as:

- Theologies of oversight and supervision within the Christian churches
- Accountability, discipline and discipleship
- Appropriate models of supervision for a theological and ecclesial context
- Appropriate use of insights from non-theological disciplines – e.g. management theory – regarding topics such as managing conflict, managing change, developing and sharing vision, and counselling regarding topics such as power, projection, transference and boundary
- Skills of mediation, negotiation and reconciliation
- Experience in being supervised and exercising a supervisory role
- Critical theological reflection upon the practice of supervision.

Extract from *Formation for Ministry within a Learning Church* (2003), London, Church House Publishing, Appendix 5.

Appendix 10
Resources for theological reflection

Aveyard, I. (1997), *God Thoughts: Engaging with the Modern World Using the Skills of Theological Reflection*, Bramcote, Nottingham, St John's Extension Studies.
This easy-to-use self-help book introduces people to theological reflection, exploring not only the issues raised by it but also methods to begin to do it.

Graham, E., Walton, H. and Ward, F. (2000), *Theological Reflection: Methods*, London, SCM.
This introduces seven different methods of theological reflection. Each method is introduced with an overview. Illustrations from history drawn from the Western tradition of the Church follow, in which the method is used, and more recent historical examples show how each method continues to inform contemporary theological reflection.

Green, L. (1980), *Let's Do Theology*, London and New York, Mowbray.
This was one of the early books introducing people to a pastoral cycle of action and reflection. In it, Laurie Green introduced people to some of the developing world and British urban examples of engaging with theology, and it is still a basic textbook on theological reflection.

Kinast, R. (1996), *Let Ministry Teach: A Guide to Theological Reflection*, Collegeville, Minn., Liturgical Press, USA.
Robert Kinast teaches theological reflection at the Center for Theological Reflection at Indianrocks Beach, Florida, and introduces and describes a step-by-step approach to help students and experienced ministers learn what their ministry teaches.

O'Connell-Killen, P. and De Beer, J. (1999), *The Art of Theological Reflection*, New York, Crossroad Publishing.
This book introduces readers to the process of theological reflection developed for an adult religious education programme called Education for Ministry. EFM originated in the USA and has had extensive development internationally. There are many groups in the United Kingdom using this four-year evening class and discussion group method. This method has good strategies for identifying and describing experience and in particular makes room for feelings, images and insight within the whole process. People who work carefully through the structured exercises

proposed in this book report that they are extremely useful and provocative.

Chadwick, C. and Tovey, P. (2000), *Growing in Ministry: Using Critical Incident Analysis*, Cambridge, Grove.
Chadwick, C. and Tovey, P. (2001), *Developing Reflective Practice for Preachers*, Cambridge, Grove.
These Grove booklets show how reflective practice can also become theological reflection.

Woodward, J. and Patterson, S. (eds.) (2000), *The Blackwell Reader in Pastoral and Practical Theology*, Oxford, Blackwell.
This became a basic textbook for people doing postgraduate work in this rather new academic discipline. There are a number of excellent articles in this book and it is an important read to surround the actual practice of theological reflection.

Further reading

On adult learning

Craig, Y. (1994), *Learning for Life: A Handbook of Adult Religious Education*, London and New York, Mowbray.

A practical and very accessible guide to adult religious education by the former National Adult Education Adviser to the Church of England.

English, L. M. (1998), *Mentoring in Religious Education*, Birmingham, Alabama, Religious Education Press.

A thorough and practical guide covering all the dimensions of mentoring for all involved in religious education both professionally and voluntarily.

On the training of curates

Burgess, N. (1998), *Into Deep Water*, Stowmarket, Kevin Mayhew.

Report by the former Director of Training in Southwell diocese on interviews with curates. Limited group of 20, but raises many important issues and records bad practice to be eschewed.

On psychological type

Duncan, Bruce, *Pray Your Way* (1993), London, Darton, Longman & Todd.

One of the most popular books exploring prayer from within the perspective of psychological type.

Francis, L. J. (2005), *Faith and Psychology: Personality, Religion and the Individual*, London, Darton, Longman & Todd.

Goldsmith, M. (1994), *Knowing Me Knowing God*, London, SPCK.

Good basic introduction to type in a religious context.

Oswald, R. and Kroeger, O. (1988), *Personality Type and Religious Leadership*, Washington DC, Alban Institute.

References

Advisory Board for Ministry (1998), *Beginning Public Ministry*, Ministry Paper 17, London, ABM.

Archbishops' Council (March 2003), *Formation for Ministry within a Learning Church*, London, Church House Publishing.

Badaracco, J. L. (2006), *Questions of Character*, Boston, HBS Press.

Bandura, A. (1986), *Social Foundations of Thought and Action: A Social Cognitive Theory*, Englewood Cliffs, New Jersey, Prentice-Hall.

Boud, D., Cohen, R. and Walker, D. (1993), *Using Experience for Learning*, Buckingham, Society for Research into Higher Education and the Open University Press.

Bramley, W. (1996), *The Supervisory Couple in Broad-spectrum Psychotherapy*, London, Free Association Press.

Briggs-Myers, I. (1980), *Gifts Differing*, Palo Alto, California, Davies-Black Publishing.

Briggs-Myers, I. and McCaulley, M. (1985), *Manual: A Guide to the Development and Use of the Myers-Briggs Type Indicator*, Palo Alto, California, Consulting Psychologists Press.

Brown, A. and Bourne, I. (1996), *The Social Work Supervisor*, Buckingham, Open University Press.

Burgess, N. (1998), *Into Deep Water*, Stowmarket, Kevin Mayhew.

Candy, P. C. (1991), *Self-direction for Lifelong Learning: A Comprehensive Guide to Theory and Practice*, San Francisco, Jossey-Bass.

Carr, W. (1985), *Brief Encounters: Pastoral Ministry through the Occasional Offices*, London, SPCK.

Chadwick, C. and Tovey, P. (2000), *Growing in Ministry: Using Critical Incident Analysis*, Cambridge, Grove Pastoral Series, 84.

Cotter, J. (1985), *Night Prayer*, Harlech, Cairns Publications.

Covey, S. (1982), *The Seven Habits of Highly Effective People*, London, Simon & Schuster.

Craig, Y. (1994), *Learning for Life: A Handbook of Adult Religious Education*, London and New York, Mowbray.

Croft, S. (2005), *Moving on in a Mission-shaped Church*, London, Church House Publishing.

Diocese of Coventry (1999), *The Training Incumbents and Curates Handbook*, Coventry, Coventry Diocese.

English, L. M. (1998), *Mentoring in Religious Education*, Birmingham, Alabama, Religious Education Press.

Formation for Ministry within a Learning Church (2003), GS 1496, London, Church House Publishing.

Foskett, J. and Lyall, D. (1988), *Helping the Helpers*, London, SPCK.

Francis, L. J. (2001), 'Personality type and communicating the Gospel', *Modern Believing*, 42(1), 32–46.

Freire, P. (1970), *Pedagogy of the Oppressed*, New York, Herder & Herder.

Gifts and Competencies: Sets of Learning Outcomes (2007), Diocese of Oxford Department of Stewardship, Training, Evangelism and Ministry.

Goldsmith, M. (1994), *Knowing Me Knowing God*, London, SPCK.

Harbidge, A. (1996), 'Those Whom D.D.O. Hath Joined Together . . .', An unpublished research paper, privately circulated by the author.

Hawkins, P. and Shohet, R. (1989), *Supervision in the Helping Professions*, Milton Keynes and Philadelphia, Open University Press.

Hess, A. K. (1980), *Psychology Supervision, Theory, Research and Practice*, New York, John Wiley & Sons.

Honey, P. and Mumford, A. (1986), *The Manual of Learning Styles*, Maidenhead, Peter Honey.

Irvine, A. (1997), *Between Two Worlds: Understanding and Managing Clergy Stress*, London, Mowbray.

Jung, C. G. (1971), *Psychological Types*, Bollingen Series, Princeton, New Jersey, Princeton University Press.

Knowles, M. S. *et al.* (1984), *Androgogy in Action: Applying Modern Principles of Adult Learning*, San Francisco, Jossey-Bass.

Kolb, D. A. (1984), *Experiential Learning*, Englewood Cliffs, New Jersey, Prentice-Hall.

Kuhrt, G. (2000), *An Introduction to Christian Ministry*, London, Church House Publishing.

Leech, K. (ed.) (1996), *Myers-Briggs: Some Critical Reflections*, Croydon, London, The Jubilee Group.

Maughan, G. (2004), 'Asking questions afterwards', *British Journal of Theological Education*, 14(2), February, 127–35.

McNeil, J. T. (ed.) (1960), *Calvin, Institutes of the Christian Religion*, Library of Christian Classics Vol. XX, London, Westminster Press.

Moon, J. (1999), *Reflection in Learning and Professional Development*, London, Kogan Page.

Morrison, T. (1993), *Staff Supervision in Social Care*, London, Pitman Publishing.

Myers, I. B. (1980), *Gifts Differing*, Palo Alto, California, Consulting Psychologists Press.

Oliver, G. (2001), 'A local success that reveals a major structural fault', *British Journal of Theological Education*, 12(1), 25–35.

Oswald, R. and Kroeger, O. (1988), *Personality Type and Religious Leadership*, Washington DC, Alban Institute.

Palmer, A., Burgess, S. and Bulmer, C. (1994), *Reflective Practice in Nursing*.

Parameters of the Curriculum and the Post-ordination Phase of IME: A Report of the Implementation Groups (2006), London, Church House Publishing.

Parsloe, E. (1999), *The Manager as Coach and Mentor*, London, CIPD.

References

Schön, D. (1987), *Educating the Reflective Practitioner: Towards a New Design for Teaching and Learning in the Professions*, San Francisco, Jossey-Bass.

Smit, T. (2002), *Eden*, The Eden Project.

Society of the Sacred Mission (1951), *Principles*, privately published by SSM.

Tight, M. (ed.) (1983), *Adult Learning and Education*, London, Croom Helm.

Tilley, D. (2006), 'Psychological Type and the Supervisory Relationship', an unpublished MPhil dissertation, Centre for Ministry Studies, University of Wales, Bangor.

Ward, F. (2005), *Lifelong Learning: Theological Education and Supervision*, London, SCM.

Williams, R. (2004), Address given at the centenary celebration of Westcott House, Cambridge, privately circulated by the author.

Wilson, A. (1999), *Promoting Wholeness: An Outline of Ministerial Supervision*, Diocese of Oxford.

Wilson, M. (1996), Handout used in a training module, privately printed and circulated.

Index